DISCOVERING ART SERIES

DISCOVERING ART SERIES

Art of the Middle Ages

adapted by Michael Batterberry

Foreword by Howard Conant

New York University

McGRAW-HILL BOOK COMPANY

New York • San Francisco • Toronto

Also in the Discovering Art Series:

NINETEENTH CENTURY ART, adapted by Ariane Ruskin

CHINESE AND ORIENTAL ART, adapted by Michael Batterberry

GREEK & ROMAN ART, adapted by Ariane Ruskin and Michael Batterberry

SEVENTEENTH & EIGHTEENTH CENTURY ART, adapted by Ariane Ruskin

TWENTIETH CENTURY ART, by Michael Batterberry

ART OF THE EARLY RENAISSANCE, adapted by Michael Batterberry

ART OF THE HIGH RENAISSANCE, adapted by Ariane Ruskin

PREHISTORIC ART AND ANCIENT ART OF THE NEAR EAST, adapted by Ariane Ruskin

Acknowledgment is hereby given to Purnell & Sons, Ltd., for the right to base this work on the text of the magazine series "Discovering Art," and to Fratelli Fabbri Editori for the right to make adaptations from the Italian text of *Capolavori Nei Secoli.*

ART OF THE MIDDLE AGES

FOREWORD

by Howard Conant, Professor and Chairman, Department of Art Education; and Head, Division of Creative Arts, New York University.

SOME OF THE most intriguing and persistent questions in man's entire history are fascinatingly dealt with in this splendid study of *Art of the Middle Ages*. And, most fortunately for readers who like to think for themselves and draw conclusions based on the best available evidence, this adaptation by Michael Batterberry literally provides us with a medieval treasure trove of new and important information, richly augmented by more than 200 illustrations in full color, which we can use in formulating our own answers to some major historical inquiries.

One of the "persistent questions" to which we refer deals with the essential concept or meaning of historic periods or eras. What is meant by the concept of medievality—the term "Middle Ages"—the popular notion of the "Dark Ages" and the designation of certain peoples as "barbarians?" A fundamental contradiction becomes immediately evident: the works of art produced by medieval peoples are anything but dark or unenlightened, and they are clearly not "barbaric." Witness, for example, the astonishingly beautiful mosaic portrait of the Byzantine empress Theodora, the artistically sophisticated Book of Kells which was produced during the so-called "Dark Ages," and the awe-inspiring, architectural mastery of the Gothic cathedrals. What this book very importantly does for us is to greatly enhance our understanding of an often-misunderstood period in history which, essentially as much as nearly any other, produced works of astonishing beauty and artistic sophistication. We thus come to better understand the concept of medievality by learning—for ourselves—that "Middle Ages" refers to a chronological *period* between the Graeco-Roman and Renaissance eras rather than to a period of "Middle" or mediocre *quality* in the arts. We thus come to better understand medieval man as one whose cultural concerns and life styles were simply different, more rugged, more earthy, more aggressive, less socially (but not less artistically) refined, than those of either classic or Renaissance man.

Another, much more subtle, but also "persistent question" raised by this book concerns the very fundamental matter of whether or not the arts of a given historical period broadly or narrowly reflect the interests and practices of its peoples. Were all—many—some—or only a few—of the Byzantine, Romanesque, and Gothic peoples as cultured and artistically enlightened as the individuals who actually created the magnificent works of art illustrated in this volume? The answer to this question—which also applies to our own lives and the society in which we live—may well be revealed to the conscientious and thoughtful reader.

CONTENTS

INTRODUCTION

IN THE WEST, the history of medieval art is essentially the same as the history of Christian art up until the time of the Italian Renaissance. In the following pages, the course of medieval art has been charted from the days of the Roman persecutions, rather than from a later point in history, so that the progress of Christian art and the development of its complicated symbols can be more clearly understood. The contributions made by Oriental and by barbarian societies to medieval European art are discussed separately, in view of their specific importance, for the full scope of medieval art can only be grasped through an examination of its many fascinating components.

Spiritual matters concerned the early Christians exclusively. They had been told, "Rejoice, for blessedness is now," and, expecting the Second Coming and the end of the world at any moment, they prepared themselves accordingly. Material or worldly things they dutifully shunned in compliance with the Gospel according to Matthew:

> Lay not up for yourselves treasures upon earth, where moth and rust doth corrupt, and where thieves break through and steal:
> But lay up for yourselves treasures in heaven, where neither moth nor rust doth corrupt, and where thieves do not break through nor steal:
> For where your treasure is, there will your heart be also.
>
> *Matt. 6:19–21*

The devout yearning of the early Christians for God's merciful deliverance and for afterlife in heaven altered the purpose of art for them. Before the Christian era, artists of the Roman Empire had principally sought to imitate the physical appearance of the natural world, and consequently their work rarely suggested more than met the eye. When they recorded the triumphs of their emperors, for example, they carved long, detailed narrative friezes and columns in the same literal storytelling manner that the Greeks had often used to portray the legends of their gods and goddesses. Like the Greeks before them, the Romans also admired physical beauty and thus depicted and venerated their gods of the spiritual world in perfected human forms.

But the Christians shared many religious laws and concepts with the Jews, and in the Ten Commandments, the worship of idolatrous images had been strictly forbidden. Confronted with the conflicting Graeco-Roman and Judaic traditions, the early Christians evolved a compromise that permitted painting and reliefs (sculpture that emerges from a flat background like a three-dimensional picture), but never freestanding statues. Freestanding statues continued to be grimly associated with images of the emperors, before which the early Christians were forced either to bow down or to die a martyr's death.

During the three centuries of repression and persecution that followed the birth of Christianity, Christian rituals reflected the solemn simplicity of the Last Supper. Baptism and the breaking of bread in memory of Christ were virtually the only ceremonies practiced by believers, for the most part in utmost secrecy. Secrecy demanded too that Christian art serve as a sign language, as a means of recognition and communication among the initiated. The crude outline of a fish, for example, hastily sketched in the air by a hand or on the ground with a stick, could immediately establish contact between two Christians uncertain of each other's spiritual loyalties. The traditional explanation for this is that in Greek, the five letters spelling fish (*ichthys*) are also the initial letters of the phrase "Jesus Christ, Son of God, Savior."

Other early symbols holding sacred meaning included the Good Shepherd ("I am the good shepherd . . . I lay down my life for my sheep.") and the peacock, whose flesh, according to legend, was incorruptible, thus symbolizing eternal life, and whose "hundred-eyed" tail suggested an all-seeing God. In Plate I-1, the small and, to us, rather odd-looking peacock approaching a beautiful glass bowl of fruit is meant to symbolize the Christian soul as it approaches the Eucharist, which offers the promise of life everlasting. This exquisite painting, equal to the finest Pompeian works of its kind, cannot, however, be considered typical

I-1. *The Grapes and the Peacock,* painting, Catacomb of Saint Sebastian, Rome.

of Early Christian art; it must be remembered that the Early Christian painters, most of whom were untrained, were forced to work patiently and stealthily, under constant fear of persecution, and we cannot therefore expect them to have created numerous masterpieces similar to those adorning the walls of luxurious Pompeian villas.

The real merit of Early Christian art lies in its strong religious conviction and its sincere emotional power rather than in any technical excellence. Through contemplation of simple Christian images, worshipers could find spiritual comfort; the artist's mission lay in recalling to the faithful Christ's teachings and message of salvation with such direct and moving force that even the humblest of converted slaves could instantly comprehend. In other words, artists now aspired to waken and illuminate the soul rather than merely to please the eye, and though their pictorial language may have been simple, even crude, it was charged with significance for the future of European art.

With love and patience the early Christian painters toiled over their sacred symbols and figures and covered hundreds of square yards of roughhewn catacomb walls, working by the dim light of little Roman oil lamps. These underground cemeteries, strongholds of primitive Christianity, are found in France, Spain, Africa, and the Danube region, but the most famous of these tunnel beneath the ground on the outskirts of Rome. Catacombs might frequently range over several levels encompassing endless passages with tombs, or *loculi,* scooped out of the dank stone walls. These tombs, where the Christian dead were buried, were sometimes framed by a painted arch such as the one shown in Plate I-2. At this early stage in Christian painting the coloring and the style remain much the

I-2. *The Twelve Apostles,* wall painting, Aurelian Hypogeum, (220–240 A.D.) Rome.

I-3. *The Good Shepherd,* wall painting, Catacomb of Priscilla, (Early Christian period) Rome.

I-4. *The Last Supper,* wall painting, Catacomb of Priscilla, (second to third centuries) Rome.

same as in pagan art. The wall painting of the Good Shepherd (Plate I-3), with its circular frame and the suggestion of trees and birds in the landscape, appears rather like a rough sketch of a Pompeian mural. So, too, does the blurred rendering of the Last Supper (Plate I-4) found in the same Roman Catacomb of Priscilla. Compare, however, the classical figure of the young shepherd with that of an *orans* (a praying man) in a wall painting (Plate I-5) from the Church of Saint John and Saint Paul in

I-5. *Praying Man* (*orans*), wall painting, Church of Saint John and Saint Paul, Rome.

I-6. *Christ, the Worker of Miracles,* painting, Catacomb of Saint Callixtus, (fourth century) Rome.

I-7. *Madonna and Child,* wall painting in the Great Cemetery, (fourth century) Rome.

Rome. The first is presented in a standard pastoral pose and bears a strong facial resemblance to the youthful Christ raising Lazarus from the dead in Plate I-6; but the *orans,* with outstretched arms and open, uplifted palms, breaks with the past to illustrate dramatically a new personal relationship with an attentive, merciful God. This moving gesture of adoration and exultation reappears frequently in Early Christian art; a further example may be studied in Plate I-7, a compelling and vivid painting of the Virgin and Child from an arched tomb recess in the Great Cemetery of Rome. On either side of the Virgin, one can make out the *chi-rho,* the monogram consisting of the Greek letters *XP,* which begin the Greek word for Christ. As we will see, the *chi-rho* was to become one of the most common symbols in Christian art.

With the Edict of Milan, or Edict of Toleration, the Emperor Constantine gave official recognition to Christianity in the year 313 A.D. Constantine's own eventual conversion to Christianity, in all probability inspired as much by practical political reasons as by religious ardor, and his momentous decision to transfer the capital of the Empire from Rome to the eastern town of Byzantium drastically altered the course of Western civilization.

The ancient Greek town of Byzantium, renamed Constantinople in honor of the Emperor, and known today as Istanbul, sprawled on either bank of the Bosphorus, the strait that acts as a partial boundary between the continents of Europe and Asia. Decidedly Oriental in its psychological atmosphere, Constantinople had decisive, immediate, and clearly recognizable effects upon the arts. The Roman concept of the emperor as the first among equals was abruptly abandoned in favor of the image of the Oriental monarch, traditionally revered by his subjects as someone half-human,

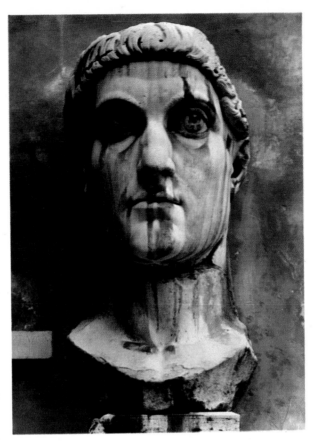

I-8. **Colossal head of Constantine, (fourth century).**

half-divine. An eerily colossal head of Constantine (Plate I-8), ten times life size, reflects this deifying attitude. The Emperor himself contributed to this change; "superhuman" perhaps best sums up the sort of effect he strove most determinedly to achieve, in regard to both himself and his capital. At court, everything was made to point up the sublime nature of his being. Gold was squandered lavishly on official trappings—imperial insignia, the crown, canopies, diadems; even the pavements were dusted with gold. Palaces and churches alike glistened with marble, silver, and ivory, stupefying the lowly beholder and impressing upon him once and for all the majestic supremacy of both God and the Emperor. Throughout the following centuries, luxury and ostentation would gain momentum at Constantinople, becoming as much of a fixture in Byzantine art as the unflinching, wide-eyed gaze, suggesting personal communication with the divine, that is seen so notably in the colossal portrait of Constantine.

Plotinus, the third-century Neoplatonic philosopher, had claimed that "a body is beautiful only if it is illuminated by the soul." Consequently, exaggerated importance was given to the expression of the eyes, the "mirror of the soul," this trend becoming increasingly obvious during the fourth, fifth, and sixth centuries.

It is known that Constantine ordered countless statues of himself to be erected in towns throughout the Empire. In at least one of these, he appeared clasping a cross in his right hand; in others, on the contrary, he was portrayed decked out in pagan emblems, such as the symbolic crown of Mithraism, an Eastern religion dedicated in part to the sacrifice of bulls.

While extending his toleration to several different faiths, Constantine determined to end the incessant theological squabblings between clashing Christian sects. To resolve their religious differences, the Emperor called upon all Christian bishops to gather together at the small city of Nicaea during the summer of 325 A.D. Those who managed or chose to attend the historic council eventually agreed on what has come to be called the Nicene Creed, an official interpretation of the Holy Trinity, giving equal theological importance to the Father, the Son, and the Holy Ghost. Constantine's approval of the Nicene Creed struck a crippling blow to the sect known as the Arians, who believed in Christ's subordination to God the Father, and whose art we shall encounter somewhat later.

Despite the new Oriental influence on official Christian art, some Churchmen tried to preserve classical Greek and Roman traditions and to reconcile them with Christian doctrine. In this respect it might be said

that the first phase of Christian art represented the final declining phase of classical art, particularly in the field of relief sculpture. The earliest existing examples of Christian relief sculpture follow the traditional Roman style of sarcophagus, or coffin, decoration. The *Sarcophagus of the Good Shepherd,* for example (Plate I-9), convincingly shows how a pagan theme could be translated directly into Christian symbolism. Pastoral scenes, cupids frolicking among vineyards, and men shouldering sacrificial lambs had been favorite subjects of Roman artists for countless generations. But now, in the Christian context, the shepherds have come to symbolize the protection of God's flocks, and the cupids become young harvesters of grapes, the vine having taken on a deep new significance as the emblem of Christ:

"I am the true vine, and my Father is
the husbandman. . . . I am the vine,
ye *are* the branches:
He that abideth in me, and I in him,
the same bringeth forth much fruit:
for without me ye can do nothing. . . .
Herein is my Father glorified, that ye
bear much fruit; so shall ye be my
disciples."

John 15: 1, 5, 8

Carved upon the sarcophagus of the Roman convert Junius Bassus (Plate I-10 is a boyish, beardless, Apollo-like Christ portrayed in the classic pose of a philosopher and teacher, scroll in hand, His feet resting upon the billowing canopy of Coelus, an ancient sky god. This is one of the first known sculptural representations of Christ. On the oval sarcophagus of Santa Maria Antica (Plate I-11), Christ appears as a child in the baptism scene at the far right; proceeding to the left we find the Good Shepherd, a philosopher (representing the person

I-9. *Sarcophagus of the Good Shepherd,* (fourth century).

I-10. *Christ Enthroned between Peter and Paul,* detail of the Sarcophagus of Junius Bassus (*c.* 359).

I-11. Oval sarcophagus of Santa Maria Antica (*c.* 270).

I-12. *Christ Presenting the Tablets of the Mosaic Law to Peter and Paul,* detail of the Sarcophagus of Saint Ambrose, (end of the fourth century). Milan.

I-13. *Christ as Teacher,* (350–360).

whose coffin this was), a praying man, and Jonah with a sea-monster version of the whale (Jonah's hair-raising adventure would remain a favorite subject of artists throughout the medieval centuries).

Christ is portrayed as philosopher-teacher once again in a detail from the *Sarcophagus of Saint Ambrose* (Plate I-12) and in a small and extremely rare fourth-century statuette (Plate I-13) that might easily be mistaken for a Greek figurine.

With Constantine's official recognition of Christianity came a pressing need for suitable houses of worship. The catacombs, having served their clandestine purpose, fell

into disuse as the first churches were consecrated in Rome, Constantinople, and all those Roman provinces that had embraced the Christian religion. Unlike pagan temples, Christian churches had to accommodate crowds of the faithful as well as provide a proper setting for the observance of holy rituals. The classic Roman basilican plan neatly provided the answer to these requirements, and it was quickly adopted as the standard architectural form for Early Christian churches not only in the western Roman Empire, but in many eastern parts as well.

A basilican church (see the ground plan

in Plate I-14), consisted of a central area called the *nave* (from the Latin word for *ship,* the ship having come to symbolize the Church of Christ), with aisles running parallel to it on either side and separated by rows of columns. The church was oriented so that the altar was at the eastern end, while at the west end there was sometimes an anteroom known as the *narthex,* where penitents might wait, or an open courtyard with cloisters (covered walks) known as the *atrium,* or both. Behind the altar, covered by a half dome projecting beyond the rectangular plan, lay the apse (see Plate I-15).

The wooden roof of the nave was always raised higher than the roofing over the aisles. In this way, windows might be fitted into the space between the two roof levels (see Plate I-16) in the zone called the *clerestory.* Marble and granite columns, often joined by arches, with finely carved capitals, were used for the nave colonnades. In some large churches a *transept,* a trans-

I-14. **Christian basilica (diagram).**

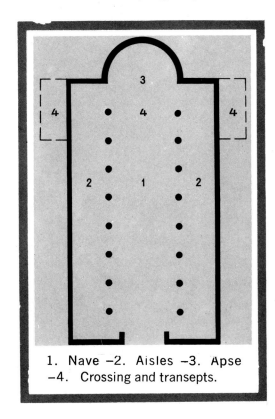

1. Nave —2. Aisles —3. Apse —4. Crossing and transepts.

verse aisle, was placed between the nave and the apse and, by extending slightly beyond either side of the nave, created a cruciform, or cross-shaped, building. Other early churches, developing from the Roman mausoleum or tomb, were round. The Church of Saint Constantia (Plate I-17) built by Constantine as a tomb for his half-sister Constantia, originally was round like other mausoleums. The barrel-vaulted ceiling of the aisle surrounding the central hall (Plates I-18, I-19) is decorated with mosaics of birds, cupids, branches, flowers, and various vessels in what appears to be a purely decorative manner (see Plate I-20); it is therefore not surprising to learn that Constantia had been a pagan before her conversion to Christianity and that it was not until 1256 that she was canonized, or made a saint, and her tomb was officially transformed into a church by Pope Alexander II. Some authorities claim, however, that in these decorative mosaics the iconography (the images and symbols representing religious subject matter) may be considered validly Christian, and they cite the peacock and the vine to support their argument.

The ancient art of mosaic reached its most spectacular heights during the Early Christian and Byzantine periods. Although the Byzantine Empire survived until the Turkish sack of Constantinople in 1453, the golden age of Byzantine art is generally acknowledged to have been seen in the fifth and the sixth centuries. Antique Roman mosaics had been purely decorative. But now, the Early Christian artists, fired by faith, brought to the old art form a deliberately awe-inspiring aura of unearthly majesty and mystery.

A mosaic is composed of countless small squarish fragments chipped from pottery, glass, marble, or other types of stone. These pieces, called *tesserae,* are embedded

I-15. Apse of the Basilica of Saint Savior, (end of fourth century) Spoleto.

closely together in wet cement to form a picture or design. The "technique," or method, of creating a mosaic might seem basically uncomplicated, although extremely time-consuming. However, in the greatest Early Christian and Byzantine mosaics, great pains were taken to vary the angles at which the tesserae were chipped and embedded so that they would reflect as much light as possible. This effect was further heightened by the increasing use of dazzling colored glass, an Eastern invention. The Romans had mainly limited their tesserae to opaque stone or pottery, but later, in addition to sparkling colored glass, gold and silver and even precious stones blazed magnificently from the walls and ceilings of religious buildings. The gold and silver tesserae were made by sandwiching metal foils between layers of clear glass; for various shades of white and gray, marble was used. In the oldest mosaics the background was white or neutral, but later it generally became a brilliant blue, and in the fifth century, especially at Ravenna, it became gold—blue and gold both symbolizing the infinite space of heaven. How complex the skill of mosaicists, or mosaic craftsmen, could become may be observed in a symbolic detail from the triumphal arch above the choir of Santa Maria Maggiore in Rome (Plate I-21). Here, in a scene where six of

I-16. **Basilica of Saint Sabina (422–432).**

I-17. Church of Saint Constantia, (first half of fourth century) Rome.

I-18. Church of Saint Constantia, (first half of fourth century) Rome.

I-19. Detail of the vaulted aisle of Saint Constantia.

I-20. Detail of vault mosaic of Saint Constantia (heavily restored).

the Disciples are represented as sheep peering up at the gates of Jerusalem, the tesserae include 33 shades of brown, 39 of green, 40 of yellow and red, 45 neutral tints, and 6 kinds of blacks and whites.

The mosaics of Rome, from the oldest to those of the sixth century, show the diminishing influence of the classical spirit. The transition from Roman naturalism to Eastern mysticism may be traced from the delightful birds and branches of Saint Constantia to the apse mosaic of Saint Pudenziana in Rome (Plate I-22), where Christ appears for the first time in the West as a regally bearded magisterial figure in the Eastern tradition, and ultimately to the awesome Christ the King, whose commanding presence, full of Oriental power and mystery, dominates the apse of Rome's Saint Cosmas and Saint Damian (Plates I-23 and I-24).

The apse mosaic of St. Pudenziana represents Christ teaching the Disciples, dressed here like Roman senators, in the heavenly Jerusalem, the free Jerusalem that "is mother to us all." Above Him rises an

I-21. Detail from the triumphal arch, Santa Maria Maggiore, (first half of fourth century) Rome.

I-22. Apse mosaic of Santa Pudenziana, (401–417) Rome.

enormous cross, the newly emphasized symbol of the Redemption, while out of the heavens loom the four beasts of Ezekiel's apocalyptic vision. In Christian iconography these winged creatures are the emblems of the four evangelists—the angel or man-faced beast being the emblem of Matthew; the lion, of Mark; the ox, of Luke; and the eagle, of John. The graceful, three-quarter postures of the Disciples still reflect a Roman naturalism, but the otherworldy feeling of the mosaic is entirely Christian in its spiritually provocative effect.

Saint Cosmas and Saint Damian, the patron saints of surgery and medicine, appear alongside the figure of Pope Felix IV in the apse of a basilica dedicated by Felix IV to the memory of these twin saints. Along with Peter and Paul they flank an Orientally "frontal" representation of Christ, which towers above them in a vast infinity of brilliantly colored clouds. The power of "frontal" figures lies in their ability to jolt the beholder into a state of spiritual awareness. Quite simply, the effect of the frontal pose is one of personal confrontation. A religious figure, when represented full face, or head on as it were, evokes a strong feeling of ceremonial authority, of direct communion between the beholder and the image itself. Since idle thoughts tend to vanish much more rapidly in face-to-face contact with an image than in the casual contemplation of a profile, no matter how forcefully drawn, "frontal" presentation would seem an ideal aid to pious meditation. Furthermore, frontality could be said to recall these words from the Book of Exodus (33:11): "And the Lord spake unto Moses face to face, as a man speaketh unto his friend."

I-23. **Apse mosaic of Saint Cosmas and Saint Damian, (sixth century) Rome.**

I-24. **Detail of apse mosaic of Saint Cosmas and Saint Damian.**

EVERYWHERE IN ITALY the development of the art of mosaic followed a similar course. In 313 A.D. the building of the churches in Milan began, the oldest still standing being San Lorenzo; a fragment of a pastoral scene, in style close to that of the mosaics in Rome, is seen in Plate II-1. The stern frontal figures of Saint Maternus and Saint Nabor (Plate II-2) from the Chapel of San Vittore in Ciel d'Oro (Saint Victor in the Golden Sky) illustrate once more the gradual progression from the naturalism of classical antiquity toward a somewhat crude yet impressive new artistic "stylization" (the deliberate simplification or distortion of natural forms). Nevertheless, the only center of mosaic which could compare favorably with Rome was Ravenna.

Ravenna lies in northeast Italy near the Adriatic coast. In Roman times it boasted its own port, its "window to the East," nearby at Classe, now silted up. After the death of Constantine, the Empire, which had earlier been divided and then reunited, again split in two. In 402 the Emperor Honorius, retreating before an invasion of Goths, transferred his court from Milan to Ravenna and made it his capital. During the next 150 years Ravenna was to thrive as a bustling building center, many of whose monuments have survived to this day.

Galla Placidia, the half sister of Honorius, herself Roman empress of the West and, for one four-year period, the hostage of Alaric, king of the Goths, was Ravenna's chief patron of art in its earliest period of greatness. The mausoleum (Plate II-3) which bears her name, but which may actually be a *martyrium,* or shrine, to Saint Lawrence, is a cruciform building of simple brick. The walls and vaults of the interior, however, are wholly lined with mosaics designed to play an integral part in the architecture, a feature typical of the finest buildings in Ravenna. The vault is patterned with symmetrical stars, looking like gilded snowflakes, against a deep blue sky. In one lunette (a semicircular area such as that seen in Plate II-4) we find for the last time in Early Christian art a portrayal of Christ, in a so-called picturesque, or naturalistic, landscape, as the beardless Good Shepherd with His flock. The regal style of Byzantium intrudes here, however, for Christ now appears in the purple and gold of an emperor rather than in simple shepherd's garb. In a detail from another lunette (Plate II-5), a symbolic hart (deer), entwined in scrolls of acanthus leaves, stoops to drink from a spring. The religious symbolism is derived from Psalm 42:1: "As the hart panteth after the water brooks, so panteth my soul after thee, O God."

In 493 Ravenna was occupied by Theodoric, king of the barbarian Ostrogoths, who unexpectedly brought Italy thirty years of peace.

Theodoric, though a Christian, supported the heretical Arians, who as we have seen, did not subscribe to the Nicene Creed, refusing to acknowledge the equal importance of Christ and God the Father, insisting that "God is the all-wise Father, and the Son is the teacher of His mysteries." For the Arians, Theodoric built a baptistery with a stiffly decorated dome (Plate II-6) that was directly copied from an earlier dome; the Twelve Apostles ring the edge of the dome,

II-1. Fragment of pastoral scene from the Chapel of Sant' Aquilino in San Lorenzo, (fifth century) Milan.

II-3. Mausoleum of Galla Placidia, (fifth century) Ravenna.

II-2. Saint Maternus and Saint Mabor from the Chapel of San Vittore in Ciel d'Oro, (late fifth century) Milan.

while at its center John baptizes Christ under the watchful eye of an incongruously classical water god, intended to personify the river Jordan.

Most importantly, Theodoric built the Church of San Martino, the name of which was later changed to Sant' Apollinare Nuovo, after the patron saint of the Catholic Franks, following the Arian's reconciliation to orthodox Catholicism in 561. A charming detail from the mosaic decorations (Plate II-7), showing three ships in the harbor of Classe, serves as the starting point for a somewhat later mosaic (Plate II-8), a procession of holy virgins bearing their crowns of martyrdom to the Virgin Mary. Aside from the glittering beauty of these mosaics, the most interesting aspect of Theodoric's church is a number of mosaic panels in which, for the first time, an attempt is made to tell the story of the life of Jesus pictorially in a series of individual episodes. Details such as Christ separating the sheep from the goats, the just from the unjust (Plate II-9), are of the utmost historical value, as they represent the introduction of instructive religious decoration, a visual method of teaching that would dominate church art for centuries to come.

Soon after the death of Theodoric, the generals of the Byzantine emperor Justinian reconquered Italy. Justinian, who liked to refer to himself as God's archpriest, celebrated his exalted position by building, among other things, an astonishing number of monuments, monasteries, and churches across the far reaches of his empire. Undisputedly the greatest of these undertakings are the magnificent Church of Hagia Sophia (Plate II-10), now a mosque, at Constantinople, considered the most outstanding single achievement in Christian art by some

authorities, and the Church of San Vitale in Ravenna, with its famous mosaic portraits of Justinian and his empress Theodora (Plates II-11, II-12).

The reign of Justinian and Theodora, the first Golden Age of Byzantium, represents a landmark not only in the arts but also in political history, in view of the extent to which these two ruthlessly ambitious personalities imposed their will, their tastes, their very image upon this important phase of civilization. Both craved glory at any price. Both managed to personify, indeed until this very day, that opulent, ornate, and treacherous way of court life traditionally associated with the word *Byzantine*. Together Justinian and Theodora established a style of life that staggered all visitors.

II-4. *The Good Shepherd,* lunette mosaic in the Mausoleum of Galla Placidia.

II-5. **Detail of a hart from lunette mosaic in the Mausoleum of Galla Placidia.**

None were prepared for the incredible display of luxury, the panoply of riches—the stiff silk robes cut on Roman lines from heavily embroidered and patterned silk, the jewels, the silver couches, the gold spittoons—nor were they prepared for the notorious "Byzantine intrigues," those complex and venomous plots and counterplots that made existence at court so harrowing for the uninitiated.

Theodora herself was a master of Byzantine intrigue, and though circumstances forced her into this role, her enthusiasm for it seems never to have diminished. The daughter of a bear-feeder in the circus, she began her astonishing career as an actress in "low comedies," a socially disgraceful occupation, and she is thought to have traveled widely before catching the eye of Justinian. In order to marry her, Justinian had to persuade his family to change the laws of the land (ironically, it is as codifier or compiler, and reinforcer of traditional Roman legal systems that he is most often remembered by history). Once installed as empress, Theodora behaved as if she had

II-6. The dome of Theodoric's Arian baptistery, (*c.* 500) Ravenna.

II-7. *Ships in the Harbor of Classe,* detail from mosaic decoration of Sant' Apollinare Nuova, (sixth century) Ravenna.

II-8. *Virgins Bearing Their Crowns of Martyrdom,* detail from mosaic decoration of Sant' Apollinare Nuovo, (sixth century) Ravenna.

II-9. *Christ Separates the Sheep from the Goats,* detail from Theodoric's mosaics in Sant' Apollinare Nuovo, (*c.* 500–526) Ravenna.

II-10. Hagia Sophia, (532–537) Istanbul.

never known any other life than that of the palace, commanding those appearing before her to prostrate themselves in a manner more humiliating than that demanded by any previous Byzantine ruler. Justinian, we are told, found her newly adopted air of majesty extremely amusing. Nevertheless it was Theodora, not Justinian, who rose to meet the greatest crisis of their reign following the Nika riots in January of 532. Evidence exists to suggest that yet another of Theodora's intrigues had led to the riots, specifically, her feud with the pious John the Cappadocian, prefect of Constantinople, whom Justinian admired. The riots, ostensibly set off by the two competing parties at the games in the Hippodrome (the By-

zantine equivalent of the Circus Maximus), grew uncontrollably into a revolution, and overnight Justinian lost his throne. Beside himself with anxiety, a fugitive in his own palace, Justinian could think of nothing else but escaping in disguise. Theodora, no stranger to poverty and disgrace, reacted scornfully to his cowardice, declaring it better to suffer a noble death than to spend the rest of one's days in ignominious safety. "The throne," she exalted, "is a glorious sepulcher," all the while plotting a successful counterrevolution which ended with the methodical slaughter of eighty thousand people in six days, most of them in the Hippodrome, where they had prematurely gathered to celebrate their victory.

In the course of the uprising, much of Constantinople was burned to the ground, thereby giving Justinian an ideal opportunity to rebuild it as he saw fit; according to Robert Payne, in *The Christian Centuries:*

He rebuilt so many churches, palaces, baths, aqueducts, cisterns, hospitals, convents, barracks, and princely houses for the nobility that in effect the old city of Constantine perished and in its place there was the city of Justinian. If the new Church of the Holy Wisdom was the greatest of his achievements, this was only because it was the largest and the most daring of many vast buildings. It was of this reconstructed city that

the poet William Butler Yeats wrote, "I think that in early Byzantium, maybe never before or since in recorded history, religious, aesthetic, and practical life were one, that architect and artifices . . . spoke to the multitude and the few alike."

Even taking into account the fact that ten thousand workmen were constantly employed, it still seems incredible that the building of Hagia Sophia, the Church of the Holy Wisdom, took only five years. The cost, however—320,000 pounds of gold—struck a disastrous blow to the imperial economy. No expense had been spared by Justinian's brilliant architects, the mathematician Anthemius of Tralles and his

II-13. Interior of Hagia Sophia.

II-14. Carved capital from a column in Hagia Sophia.

assistant, Isidore of Miletus, both Greeks from Asia Minor.

The characteristic feature of Byzantine church architecture is the dome or group of domes. The dome of Hagia Sophia, originally painted gold, measures a breathtaking 107 feet across, covers the central interior square, and is flanked to east and west by lower half domes. From the nave, arcades open into the aisles (see Plate II-13). The columns of these arcades have richly carved capitals (see Plate II-14) that loosely follow the Ionic style. The lower part of the walls is sheathed in many subtle shades of rare marbles brought from every corner of the Empire; the original mosaics were studded with precious stones and most

probably included monumental portraits of Justinian and Theodora, but by now they have all but gone. Justinian, himself a practicing architect, supervised every aspect of Hagia Sophia's construction and design. At the formal consecration ceremonies of his architectural masterpiece, the Emperor, barely able to control his pride, reportedly cried out: "Glory be to God who hath thought one worthy to accomplish such a work as this; O, Solomon, I have outshone thee!"

The Church of San Vitale (Plate II-15), founded some time before 534, was completed for Justinian and consecrated in 547. Built of brick like other Ravenna churches, the severely plain exterior tells little of its

II-15. **Church of San Vitale, (consecrated in 547) Ravenna.**

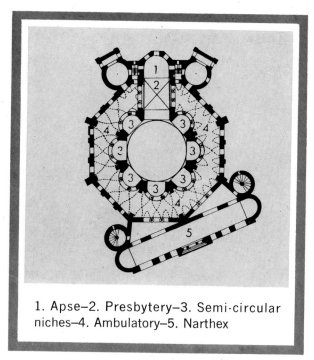

1. Apse—2. Presbytery—3. Semi-circular niches—4. Ambulatory—5. Narthex

II-16. **Plan of the Basilica of the Church of San Vitale at Ravenna.**

complex plan (Plate II-16), what exterior decoration there was has gone, which makes the contrast with the splendid mosaics and marbles inside all the greater. Basically, the building is a domed central octagon with a surrounding ambulatory, a sheltered walkway, and a gallery above. The central octagon is separated from the ambulatory not by simple arches but by open niches, each formed by three arches. Space and wall, column and arch alternate in a continual play of curves, with the colorful marble and mosaic decoration forming an integral part of the whole.

The full significance of the Church of San Vitale must be assessed in a variety of lights. First of all, we find here, in this jewel of Justinian's "overseas" building program, a unique fusion of Western and Eastern artistic styles.

In the San Vitale mosaics (see Plate II-17), Christ, His triple-branched halo representing the Holy Trinity, is still portrayed in the Western manner: beardless, youthful, seated

upon the universe, and offering His symbolic martyr's crown to Saint Vitalis (San Vitale). At His left, the Bishop Ecclesius holds a model of the Church of San Vitale. Eastern influence is represented in part by intricately carved capitals (see Plate II-18) that look like sculptured drawing.

Whether or not Justinian and Theodora actually traveled to Ravenna for the church's consecration is not known, nor is it of vital importance. The question does arise, though, as to the accuracy of their likenesses in the mosaics representing them (Plates II-11, II-12). Did the Emperor and the Empress actually pose for the original drawings, or cartoons, as the plans for mosaics are called, or are these merely standardized images of bejeweled potentates? The strong individuality of the mosaic faces, reflecting the Western tradition of realistic portraiture, leads us hopefully to believe that the artists actually knew their subjects, that we see Justinian and Theodora as they really appeared, he with all his sensuous pride, she with all her intensity, intelligence, and cool self-assurance. Yet the identical aloofness of the church officials and the courtiers in the ranks of an Eastern pageant portrayed in other San Vitale mosaics (see Plate II-19) leads us to wonder if the essential purpose of the mosaics was not simply to immortalize Justinian and Theodora on a plane close to that of Christ Himself.

In other words, are these symbols or people? And if they are mere human beings, are they not treading on dangerous ground by brazenly establishing themselves, halos and all, as God's regal representatives? Granted they are portrayed in the act of presenting votive gifts to the church, but faced with their expressions of calm arrogance, their total lack of humility, one could as easily be led into thinking that they were receiving rather than paying tribute.

II-17. Apse mosaic from the Church of San Vitale.

II-11. Mosaic portrait of Justinian I from the Church of San Vitale.

II-18. Carved capital from the Church of San Vitale.

II-12. **Mosaic portrait of the Empress Theodora from the Church of San Vitale.**

Here, for all time, the essence of Byzantine grandeur and conspicuously ornate majesty is captured, suitably enough, in little chips of gold and silver, glass and colored stone.

The Byzantine Empire's greatest period of prosperity encompassed the fifth and sixth centuries and reached its highest peak during the reign of Justinian. In the sixth century, revenues flowed in from North Africa, southern Europe, and the East, and imperial patronage, well organized by a cultured civil service, encouraged the development of art. Architects and mosaicists were kept working furiously to satisfy the Byzantine craving for grandeur, while countless other skilled artists and artisans from the breadth of the Empire migrated to the workshops of the capital in answer to the insatiable demands for luxury and ostentation.

Except for the occasional imperial portrait, such as the marble head, most likely of Theodora in Plate II-20, sculpture in the round was uncommon. Frescoes, (murals painted on wet plaster) and paintings were popular, however, and though they have not survived, we know that portraiture flourished in the sixth century and that Justinian decorated his palace with frescoes of contemporary chariot races. Much of what has survived belongs to the so-called minor arts—ivories, jewels, silks, gold and silverware, illuminated manuscripts, and enamels. This is not to say that such arts and crafts were thought of as inferior to the "major arts" of architecture, sculpture, and painting; on the contrary, the finest creations of the workshops, prized as visible symbols of wealth, taste, or religious devotion, were regarded as masterpieces by the Byzantines.

Among the most refined of these objects are the ivories and jewelry, one example of the latter being the equestrian figure of an emperor, perhaps Justinian, seen in

II-19. Mosaic of Emperor and Empress with attendants, from the Church of San Vitale.

Plate II-21. The Byzantines' sensitivity to the subtle color variations of ivory is revealed in this sixth-century appreciation: "Sometimes the ivory has the choicest tint of a pale crocus, sometimes the tint of the light creeping round the pointed horns of a new-born moon." The magnificent gold jewel in the form of an eagle, shown in Plate II-22, was found as far afield as Skåne, Sweden, and testifies to the Byzantine feeling for contrasting textures, in this case filigreed and granulated gold, as well as to their love of symmetry. Together, these splendidly ornamental specimens exemplify once more the sense of majesty and opulence we have come to expect of Byzantine art.

II-20. Marble portrait head, probably of the Empress Theodora, (fifth century) Milan.

II-21. Equestrian figure of an emperor, Byzantine ivory (early sixth century).

II-22. Gold jewel in the form of an eagle, Byzantine (c. 500).

Barbarian Art

III-1. **Runic stone from Skansen, (after 300 A.D.) Sweden.**

BETWEEN THE THIRD and the fifth centuries, the West was gradually engulfed by Lombards, Visigoths, and Ostrogoths, marauding warrior tribes who, having succeeded in first undermining and then destroying the Roman Empire, were in turn driven on by the last and most terrible of the invaders, the Huns from central Asia.

After 476 A.D. the Roman emperors and their system of government disappeared entirely, and the Christian Church, as heir to the Roman Empire, assumed the position of central authority following the final breakdown of the old governmental machinery. Memory of Roman greatness faded as cities were deserted or occupied by barbarian tribes such as the Scythians, Sarmatians, and Goths. The last brought fresh ideas and forms to the decorative art that the Celts had earlier evolved in central and western Europe, and from these different strains the Germanic style emerged.

By necessity, the art of wandering tribes had to be limited to the crafting of easily portable and preferably valuable objects, such as jewelry and ornate weapons and animal trappings. The Germanic style is seen at its best in goldsmiths' work and other metalwork (especially in jewelry), as well as in the mysterious runic stones of Scandinavia (see Plates III-1–III-2). Stylized animals and birds delighted barbarian artist-craftsmen as much as intricate abstract designs. They reveled in meshes and whirlpools of swirling, interlacing lines and loved to cover the entire surface of a shield or helmet or ornament with circles, spirals, triangles, and overlapping scrolls and knots.

A sense of design was instinctive and spontaneous in the Germanic peoples, and later their lively, flexible line would reappear incessantly, together with their contempt for empty spaces, in medieval metalwork, stonework, and illuminated manuscripts. In the course of time these tribes settled down in Germany, the Balkans, Spain, Britain, and France, pushing the Celts farther west into Brittany, Ireland, Cornwall, and Wales. During the sixth century, Goths and Lombards spread over the north and the central areas of Italy, intermarrying with the local population, and leaving as artistic evidence of their arrival much jewelry made of gold, glass paste, and colored stones. The brooch in the form of a stylized eagle

III-2. **Barbarian brooch in the form of an eagle,** (fifth century).

tribes used in inscribing metal and bone. They may be letters belonging to a primitive alphabet, but more likely they are magical signs. Other such runic stones may be covered by figures and groups, sometimes lifelike, sometimes fantastic; to this day they remain a tantalizing puzzle to which the clue is lost.

In the art of the Angles and the Saxons, Britain's barbarian conquerors, geometric patterns, interlacing lines, and animal motifs were also being used in metalwork such as jewelry with great ingenuity and a strong sense of design. The discovery of the Sutton Hoo royal burial ship on the East Anglian coast of Britain in 1939 was of major importance. Though only the ashen outlines of the burial craft remain in the damp earth to indicate its original shape, its contents are still being meticulously catalogued. They reveal the richness, variety, and technical brilliance of Anglo-Saxon applied art in pagan times. A purse lid from the burial ship (Plate III-5), with gold frame, fittings, and ornamental plaques, that was decorated with garnets and glass mosaics shows that Saxon goldsmiths practiced enameling, a technique otherwise found only in Celtic work in northern Europe. The animal and human figures in the plaques are especially interesting, for two of them show ducks being seized by birds of prey, a Scythian motif; the other two show stylized men standing between symmetrical pairs of animals, a decorative theme that can be traced back to ancient Mesopotamian art.

In the treasures unearthed at Sutton Hoo, Anglo-Saxon and Celtic traditions appear to be fused. Interlacing patterns, spirals, and animal shapes were all used in Celtic as well as Germanic art, as may be seen in Plate III-6 in the seething design of a gold buckle from the vanished ship.

in Plate III-2 is an example of their work.

Other examples of the barbarian's art reproduced here include a wonderfully ornate gold medallion from Sweden (Plate III-3), the central pattern of which has been inspired by the idea of an emperor on horseback, and a sinister, badly rusted bronze helmet (Plate III-4). The upright runic stone in Plate III-1, one of many found in Sweden and Norway, is inscribed with the same *runes,* or characters, that Germanic

III-3. Gold medallion, Germanic (450–550).

These two ancient and living traditions, Celtic and Anglo-Saxon, contributed equally to the art that produced the Book of Durrow and the Book of Kells in Ireland, and the Lindisfarne Gospels in Northumbria (the northeastern section of England). It was Christianity that provided the immediate inspiration for these works; the new religion had been brought to Irish shores by monks from Syria and from Egypt, the country in which Christian monasteries originated.

Art of the Irish Monks

The earliest monks lived as hermits either in the desert or in solitude in caves or ramshackle huts, eventually banding together here and there to build chapels, churches, and other simple halls for communal use. Called *cenobites,* these holy recluses refused to relinquish their individual huts and continued to pass most of their time alone, occupied as they saw fit. The kind of organized monasticism we associate today with the Middle Ages did not come into being until 530 A.D., the year Saint Benedict founded his monastery at Monte Cassino in northern Italy under the jurisdiction of the Roman Church.

Early in the fifth century, the island of Lerins near Marseilles was chosen by the Egyptian monks as their first European home; from there missionaries were dispatched to Ireland to convert the Scoti, as

III-4. **Barbarian bronze helmet (sixth to ninth centuries).**

III-5. **Purse lid from the royal burial ship at Sutton Hoo, England, Anglo-Saxon (*c.* 655).**

III-6. Gold buckle from Sutton Hoo, (seventh century) Anglo-Saxon.

III-7. Page from the Book of Kells, Celtic (Irish) (c. 800).

41

III-8. **Illuminated page from the Lindisfarne Gospels, Celtic-Anglo-Saxon (c. 700).**

Celtic art at its most intricately abandoned; one can spend hours chasing the serpentine lines and tiny human faces and figures about the page.

The Lindisfarne Gospels (see Plate III-8), a famous manuscript of the early eighth century, is the work of Irish monks living on the isle of Lindisfarne (Holy Island) off the coast of Northumberland. The pattern work is, once again, fascinatingly complex and varied, using the Celtic motifs of spiral, lozenge, and intertwined birds and animals along with geometric motifs found in Saxon jewelry.

Saint Augustine had been responsible for introducing books to Anglo-Saxon Christendom in the sixth century, and in the eighth century, Abbot Benedict Biscop, a successor, traveled several times to Rome to bring more precious examples back to Britain. Despite this reverence for books from Rome, however, the work of the Irish monks was highly original, in addition to being technically brilliant.

The mushrooming of the monastic system in western Europe was in part due to the successful missionary work of these Irish monks, who sent emissaries to Scotland, Germany, France, Italy, and Switzerland; abroad the natives nicknamed them "the striped ones," in reference to their loudly patterned, brightly colored robes. But their specific influence was not lasting; since the turn of the seventh century, bitter conflict had existed between the Irish monks and the Roman Benedictines as to ritual and the conversion of Saxon rulers. The Benedictines triumphed following a climactic clash at the Synod of Whitby in 664, and it was then that the Irish Church, determined to salvage her lost prestige, directed all efforts to the production of such widely admired works as the books of Kells and Durrow and the Lindisfarne Gospels.

the Irish were then known, and to build more monasteries. In the monasteries along the Irish coast and on the island of Iona, the monks dedicated themselves equally to prayer and to work. Their supreme accomplishment is to be found in illuminated copies of the Gospels such as the Book of Kells. Plate III-7 shows the Greek monogram *XPI,* the first three letters of the Greek *Christos,* as it appeared in the Book of Kells—dazzling and bewildering in its convulsive abstract patterns. This is

Carolingian Art

THE FRANKS, by the eighth century, had become the most powerful of the barbarian peoples in western Europe. Having forcefully subdued their neighbors, the Lombards, the Avars, and the Saxons, the Franks made swift progress toward a new civilization under their legendary king, Charlemagne, or Charles the Great (742–814). The word *Carolingian,* from the Latin for Charlemagne, *Carolus Magnus,* is used to describe the inspired culture that, through Charlemagne's determined prodding and wise choice of advisors, burst into life at this time. What it brought to Europe is known as the Carolingian Renaissance.

Charlemagne, no matter how enlightened his administration may have been, remained a true barbarian. A merciless warrior and despot, he stopped at nothing, not even the massacre of thousands of hapless hostages, in his militant drive to bring about Europe's total conversion by the sword. Physically, he was indeed entitled to the name "Charles the Great," for he stood almost seven feet tall and his strength was prodigious. He took eight wives, fathered fourteen children, and died at the age of seventy-five at a time when the average life expectancy fell somewhere between thirty and thirty-five, or alarmingly less in years of war, famine, or epidemic. Most historians claim that Charlemagne was illiterate and could only manage to sign his name; others insist that he could read Latin and that until the end of his reign, he took writing tablets to bed with him in the optimistic hope that practice might make his writing passable if not precisely perfect.

Rough and fearless, Charlemagne demanded at all times the complete satisfaction of his restless ambitions. He wished to live as befitted a conqueror of his singular stature, and toward the creation of a brilliant court and capital he directed the same fierce energy that had brought whole nations to their bleeding knees. A sign of Charlemagne's true greatness, and his sharp intuition, was his willingness to delegate authority to others better educated than he. Most prominent among the battalion of intellectuals, artists, and artisans whom Charlemagne summoned to his capital at Aachen (Aix-la-Chapelle) were the scholar Alciun of York, a classicist, a reformer of handwriting, and organizer of the Palatine, or Palace, School, and Eginhard, official biographer to the King, architect, collector of antique art, and director of the royal workshops of artisans.

Alciun's contribution to Western civilization cannot be overemphasized, for it was he who organized the monastic scriptoria, the famous manuscript workshops in which great works of classical literature were copied and thus preserved for future generations of mankind. Alciun was furthermore responsible for the invention and perfection of the Carolingian, or Caroline, miniscule script, a form of writing based on the Roman alphabet and later adapted during the Italian Renaissance to the printing press. Carolingian miniscule continues to form the basis of our finest modern calligraphy, or penmanship; an example appears in a detail from the Utrecht Psalter in Plate IV-1.

It was the intention of the Palatine School to emulate all that had been great

IV-1. **Detail from the Utrecht Psalter** (*c.* 832).

in the classic tradition, but within a devoutly Christian framework, innocent of any pagan references. Charlemagne himself attended religious services three times a day and spent fortunes financing monasteries and other religious buildings. One major windfall of booty came into Charlemagne's hands when he crushed the Avars, a Mongoloid race of professional warriors who wore their hair in pigtails and who, for several centuries, had been heavily rewarded by the Byzantine emperors for their far-ranging protective services. Priceless caches of gold and precious stones, ivories, silverware, and heavy silk robes were confiscated and converted into funds both for the glorification of God and, following his coronation in Rome by Pope Leo III in the year 800, for the glorification of Charlemagne, Emperor of the Holy Roman Empire and Protector of Christendom.

Charlemagne dreamed of a lasting peace under one God for all the peoples of western Europe; he craved greatness in the tradition of the Caesars and embarked on a series of high-minded programs, including, for the first time in history, a plan whereby all the subjects of his empire would receive a free education. Like all great conquerors before him, he called upon architects to immortalize his greatness in monumental terms. Atop a hill in Aachen a great palace arose with bright red walls gleaming beneath an enormous bronze eagle with widespread wings. A covered colonnade, four hundred feet long, ran down the hillside and connected the palace with the Palatine Chapel (Plate IV-2), the entire project being conceived and executed between 798 and 805 by the royal architect Eginhard. The octagonal plan of the Palatine Chapel is based on that of San Vitale at Ravenna (see Plate II-16), but on the whole, most other Carolingian churches continued to follow the basilican plan. In the forecourt was displayed a statue of Theodoric on horseback that had been unceremoniously looted from Ravenna, and to further the imperial effect, a marble throne, from which Charlemagne could see and be seen by all, loomed out of the chapel gallery above the heads of the priests. Eginhard reports that the Emperor insisted the chapel be kept immaculate and constantly warned the sextons not to allow anything or anyone dirty to enter.

Aachen soon became the center of the Western world, surpassing Constantinople in power and approaching it in magnificence. Yet Charlemagne's capital remained unique, in the sense that no other city of the slightest importance grew up in western Europe during the early Middle Ages, that is to say, roughly the time elapsing between the barbarian invasions and the eleventh century.

Each day ambassadors, travelers, wandering minstrels, artisans, and the like poured into Aachen from every direction, having come on foot, on horseback or by mule train. The Caliph Haran al Rashid, making advantageous peace with Charlemagne, sent envoys and caravans from Baghdad laden with fabulous and exotic gifts—patterned silks, Oriental jewelry, perfumes, spices (pepper was then more valuable to Europeans than was the finest fur), a water clock with figures that emerged every hour, a live elephant in full regalia, and, to the Carolingians' excitement and fascination, a palatial tent honeycombed with countless rainbow-colored apartments.

Byzantine works, too, came to the court at Aachen. Ambassadors sent by the eastern Roman emperor brought presents of silks and ivory, which were treasured and imitated. Sometimes copies were made directly of Byzantine models, but often the resemblance between Eastern and Western ivories, and between these and the miniatures that inspired many of them, is due to their common inheritance of Early Christian and late classical art.

Many Byzantine artists had fled to western Europe when, in 726, all religious art, including paintings, mosaics, and statues, was forbidden by the eastern emperor as a result of a raging controversy over the worship of images. Those condemning religious art were known as the Iconoclasts, literally "the image-smashers"; in truth, money and power lay at the heart of the matter, since many government officials felt that the monasteries profited excessively from pilgrims who came to pay tribute to holy pictures and relics owned by the monks. In any case, the Byzantine style was kept alive in Italy by refugee artists who were left free to paint or produce mosaics in their traditional style, and their influence on local artists was eventually transmitted throughout the Holy Roman Empire.

IV-2. **The Palatine Chapel at Aachen (798–805).**

Inevitably, this cross-pollination of cultures at Aachen had a rich and fertilizing effect upon art; bearing this in mind, one can easily understand why Carolingian art is so often termed "eclectic," meaning that it borrows freely from many different established styles. The melding of disparate traditions into a distinctive new style is called an artistic synthesis, and this is what Carolingian art undoubtedly achieved.

The Carolingian figurative style is seen most clearly in the art of manuscript illumination. Under the direction of Alciun of York, as has been mentioned, great workshops, attached to the imperial palace at Aachen, were established, and they were kept constantly busy. Soon several different schools of manuscript illumination sprang up at Metz, Tours, Rheims, St. Gall, and elsewhere. These schools, artistically and regionally designated as the Ada, Liuthard, Rheims, and Metz groups, each produced work of an individual character. The Ada style, with its closed architectural settings, one example of which can be seen in Plate IV-3, tends to be rather hard and monumental. This page from an evangelistary, a book of the Gospels from which a priest reads to his parrish, written by the clerk Godescalc for Charlemagne and his wife Hildegarde in 781–783, is taken from the earliest manuscript of the Ada group produced at the Palatine School. The figure of Christ is painted in the Byzantine manner: frontal, stiff, with large, staring eyes. Christ remains beardless, in the Western tradition, and is shown seated on a throne, holding a book, much as ancient philosophers had been depicted. The interlacing spirals and other formal motifs in the border can be traced directly to Germanic or Celtic art. Other pages are devoted to portraits of the four Evangelists seated at their desks, pens in hand, composing the Gospels; again these portraits show the architectural background characteristic of the Ada group.

One of the most interesting works of Carolingian narrative art, the Utrecht Psalter, which we mentioned earlier, was written at Rheims about 832. In style the illustrations (see Plate IV-1) differ sharply from those of Godescalc's evangelistary. These exceptional line drawings, sketched in rapid, nervous, swirling pen strokes, bubble with life and unexpected, intriguing details, such as in one drawing, not shown here, where an angel roughly shakes God awake as He lies in His bed.

Carolingian jewelers, too, worked in dazzling detail; this love of small refinements typifies all of great Carolingian art and as we have seen reflects the need of that civilization's nomadic warrior ancestors for easily transported valuables. The splendid "Iron Crown" shown in Plate IV-4 is actually made of gold *repoussé,* gold hammered into a raised design from the reverse side, and is set with precious stones and enamel in the *cloisonné* technique. This method, much used by barbarian craftsmen, entails the fastening of small metal ridges, usually of gold, to a metal background. Compartments of these raised metal ridges are called *cloisons.* Stones such as garnets, extremely popular in the Middle Ages, pieces of colored glass, and of enamel paste were then fitted in to the compartments, the edges of which remain visible on the surface as part of the overall design. The gems of the Iron Crown follow the Carolingian taste for polished but uncut stones, as will be noted again in a gold *repoussé* book cover embellished with figures and scenes in gold relief (Plate IV-5).

IV-3. **Page from the Godescalc Evangelistary (781–783).**

IV-4. The Iron Crown (ninth century).

IV-5. Gold *repoussé* book cover (870).

The extraordinarily ornate object appearing in Plate IV-6 is a Carolingian reliquary of the tooth of Saint John. Relics of saints and martyrs had been collected and cherished by devout Christians since the earliest days of the Roman persecutions, and as the centuries passed, faithful worshipers came to attribute miraculous powers to these pieces of bone and hair and splinters of wood. Pope Gregory the Great, who, in the sixth century, had bestowed the Church's official approval upon painting as a tool of religious instruction, had been a great believer in relics. Frequently he would send gifts of hair and bone to kings and Oriental potentates, or, as he did on one occasion, a small key made from Peter's chains. The Eastern monarchs, however, found it difficult to grasp the significance of these holy objects, since the East concerned itself more with the abstract than the material aspects of religion. But relics held great meaning for the West, and reliquaries designed to hold or display such holy objects were fashioned from an endless variety of materials. Sometimes, if the holy object was something like an arm or a finger, the reliquary was shaped in the form of the relic itself.

A piece of the famous "Charioteer silk" taken from the tomb of Charlemagne at Aachen appears in Plate IV-7. The silk, probably woven in Constantinople, has been assigned to the sixth century, but as it is improbable that Charlemagne would have been buried with a piece of silk two centuries old, some authorities now feel that it is more likely to be of the late eighth century.

In architecture, Frankish and German builders of the Carolingian period began to work in stone instead of wood. Next to the Palatine Chapel, which was built of stone, Charlemagne's contemporaries considered the greatest achievement of his reign to have been a great wooden bridge that spanned the Rhine. However, it was in stonework that the Carolingians were to make their greatest contribution. Architects continued to draw heavily on Roman and Byzantine models, but they built in a new way, with monumental severity and massive walls, which were to be the chief characteristics of the future romanesque style. Medieval masonry begins in Carolingian architecture, and a whole group of Romanesque buildings derive from the Palatine Chapel at Aachen. Carolingian architecture was able to blend classical and barbarian elements successfully, as can be seen particularly well in the Gateway to the Abbey of Lorsch in Germany (Plate IV-8). The massive arcade, the Corinthian columns, and the row of pilasters above them are all borrowed from Roman models, but the ebulliently checkered facade, or surface, is purely Germanic in origin.

The wall paintings in Carolingian churches and palaces referred to in writings of that time have disappeared or have been drastically altered, with only a few exceptions. What does remain to us of the art of Charlemagne's time, however, continues to give ample evidence of the richness of the Carolingian synthesis.

IV-6. **Reliquary of the tooth of Saint John** (late ninth century).

IV-7. **A piece of the "Charioteer Silk"** (sixth to eighth century ?).

IV-8. **Gateway to the Abbey of Lorsch,** (late eighth century) Germany.

CHARLEMAGNE DIED IN 814 survived by only one son. Lacking the old warrior's genius as a ruler, his son and the later successors to the throne were unable to stem the strife that was disintegrating his empire. Not until 962, when Otto I, known as Otto the Great (912–973), had himself crowned emperor at Rome, was the Holy Roman Empire reestablished, signaling the birth of the Ottonian Dynasty. Ottonian art modeled itself upon the Carolingian style although, generally speaking, it owed less to classical tradition. The figure of Christ enthroned found upon a carved ivory plaque from Metz (Plate V-1), for example, bears a striking resemblance to Godescalc's Christ in Plate IV-3.

Political power makes itself felt in much Ottonian art, particularly in numerous portraits of emperors, kings, princes, and their families. Likewise, Eastern artistic traditions are in evidence, for Otto II (955–983) married a Byzantine empress, Theophano, and quite logically, Eastern styles asserted themselves upon court taste. Plate V-2 shows a portrait of their son, the boy emperor Otto III (he died at the age of twenty-two), regally enthroned, wearing Byzantine-inspired robes and clasping the orb and scepter, as he receives homage from many nations. This formal painting served as a prototype for many later medieval portraits of kings.

A notable progress toward abstraction and away from naturalism in Ottonian art may be recognized immediately in a spellbinding miniature painting of Saint Luke (Plate V-3) taken from a manuscript copy of the Gospels made for Emperor Otto III.

V-1. *Christ in Glory,* ivory plaque from Metz, Ottonian (tenth century).

Here the intense spiritual thoughts of an evangelist are no longer represented simply by a book lying in the figure's lap; instead, they burst forth from his head and outstretched finger tips in a dramatic explosion consisting of prophets, angels, and Luke's personal symbol, the winged ox (wings

v-2. Official portrait of Emperor Otto III, Ottonian (late tenth century).

v-3. *The Revelation of Saint Luke,* Ottonian. (*c.* 1000).

signify divine mission, while the ox, a sacrificial animal of the Jews, symbolizes Christ, the "true" sacrifice). Surrounded by a *mandorla* (the Italian word for "almond," hence an almond-shaped frame) and seated on the Rainbow of the Alliance, symbol of spiritual union, Luke holds the Earthly City in his lap. His figure is poised in space and the whole composition seems weightless. Luke, incidentally, is the patron saint of painters, and legends persist that, although known primarily as a practicing physician, he executed several portraits of Jesus and the Virgin Mary.

As The Year 1000 drew close, dark and menacing prophecies spread deep anxiety throughout western Europe. A universal feeling of uncertainty and an oppressive sense of sinfulness fell like a pall. Many felt that the day of reckoning, the dreaded doomsday, as foretold in the Apocalypse, would come at the end of the first millennium after the birth of Christ, and, quaking, the people despaired.

For centuries after the collapse of the Roman Empire, barbarian invasions had inflicted death and devastation; cities had been razed and the ravaged, deserted fields could not possibly produce sufficient food to feed the population. There could be neither satisfaction for the present nor hope for the future. The Church of this period, deeply corroded by superstition, had little success in reassuring troubled souls.

By present standards, life in the Middle Ages, even that of the nobility, would be considered extremely harsh. Self-reliance was deemed not so much a virtue as a means of survival and had to be mastered early in life; by the time a child reached his fifth or sixth birthday, he was expected to look after himself as an adult. Although knights and the nobility scorned manual labor, leisure was foreign to them, for there were always wars to be waged or animals to be hunted or family honor to be avenged. But like the peasants, many of the nobility slept on straw, wore the same garment year after year, and seemed otherwise oblivious to discomfort. Beyond soldiering and hunting, the nobles had little other aim in life. As for the peasants, little is known of their daily life for the simple reason that those who could write found the subject too in-

significant to waste time upon.

Danger lurked everywhere; famine and epidemic, fire and charging wild beasts, droughts and floods. Physical strength was man's only assurance of freedom, and, pursuing this end, he left the luxury of learning to Churchmen, who, generally speaking, constituted the only educated class.

Schools other than those directed by the Church simply did not exist, and consequently it fell to the clerics, recruited from all walks of life, to keep civilization alive throughout the centuries of darkness and invasions. The notion still persists that monks in the Middle Ages occupied themselves almost exclusively with fasting, praying, copying and illuminating manuscripts, and tending their vineyards or wine cellars. But we must correct this legendary picture by adding that all important professional services were also performed by clerics—they were the doctors, lawyers, accountants, engineers, architects, and diplomats. Charity, too, was left exclusively to the administration of the Church, with the possible exception, of course, of the scraps and bones which the nobles tossed to the dogs and ravenous beggars that snarled at each other beneath the long trestle tables of the great dining halls.

Popular religion, that is to say, religion as it was actually practiced by the people, bore many resemblances to paganism. Old superstitions were incorporated into Christian rituals and beliefs by the peasantry, who happily occupied themselves with endless harvest festivals, pageants and ceremonies on feastdays, penitential processions, and the like. The clergy rarely bothered to read, let alone explain, the Gospels to their flocks, although most people knew intimately the story of Jesus and the lives of the saints and were familiar with Old Testament stories.

When at last the fateful year 1000 had receded, without bringing, as many people had feared, final catastrophe, a new spirit manifested itself, bringing a renewed sense of destiny. And at about the same time, migrating barbarian tribes started to settle in definite geographical areas, forming themselves into more organized settlements and beginning to make important contributions to medieval society.

Fiefs and kingdoms gradually developed, and along with them, an organized society capable of supervising the resurgence of trade and agriculture. New religious orders sprang up, and the Church now campaigned to dispel pagan elements and folk superstitions with concrete Christian teachings.

A wave of spiritual energy surged across western Europe and brought with it a flowering of artistic expression in what is today France, England, Spain, and Germany. This new and severely striking phase of art is known as the Romanesque. The term *Romanesque,* coined by the French archaeologist Charles de Gerville in the last century, was originally intended to identify a style and period by linking Rome and ancient architectural traditions with Western architecture of the fifth through thirteenth centuries. By now, however, the Romanesque period (known in England as the Norman period) has been restricted roughly to the eleventh and twelfth centuries.

In its infancy, the Romanesque period succumbed to a fever of church-building. A monk named Raoul Glaber, "Raoul the Bald," writing in imperfect Latin sometime about 1048, recalled in his chronicles this childhood impression:

It happened that in the years that followed the year 1000 all over the universe, but particularly in Italy and Gaul, we bore witness to the rebuilding of churches, even if there was no need of it, and the greater number were well built and did not need such care. Each Christian community resolved to rival the others in building sanctuaries more noble than those of its neighbors. . . . It was as if the world, anxious to cast off her rags, was now dressed everywhere in a beautiful white robe of churches.

The Romanesque period's link with the classical past of Rome is inadvertently described in the phrase "rebuilding of churches"; for the most part those churches that had survived adhered to the basilican plan, and in rebuilding them, men of the Middle Ages were thus following classical styles.

However, the aspirations and spiritual intensity of the period at its peak are expressed most aptly by the cathedral, the monumental achievement of Romanesque architects and masterbuilders. The new cathedrals were quite distinct from the huge basilicas and simple churches of the Carolingian period. The Romanesque church, characterized by heavy masses and powerful walls, sturdy columns and rhythmic arches, did not insist on an immediate confrontation with God; rather, by slow degrees, it drew the believer on, preparing him for the central mystery of the altar. The calmly majestic, luminous nave of the Church of Saint Magdalen at Vézelay (Plate VI-1) reflects this deeply moving concept.

Builders of the Romanesque period generally relied upon traditional and time-proven methods of construction that probably represented to a great extent the practices of Roman times. Ingenuity as well as courage was required to raise and lay

VI-1. Interior of the Church Saint Magdalen of Vézelay (twelfth century).

stone at a dangerous height above the ground, particularly when wooden scaffolding and primitive lifting devices were all the early Romanesque engineers had at their command. The scale on which they chose to build, by reason of its very size and soaring vision, called for the perfection of efficient new building techniques, and specialists were often hired from Byzantium and Rome to give advice. Ambitious architects in western Europe soon began experimenting with vaulted stone ceilings, which, besides presenting a more unified aspect than wooden ones did, lessened the risk of fire, the scourge of medieval churches. The problem of vaulting seems to have been mastered in several centers at approximately the same time—at Cluny in Burgundy, at Speyer, or Spires, in Germany, and at Durham in England (see map in Plate VI-2).

The transitional ribbed vault, the outstanding structural achievement of the Romanesque period, was a stronger type of vault, was easier to build, and visually clarified the design of architectural volumes. Probably the earliest example is to be found at Durham Cathedral (Plate VI-3). The evolution of the ribbed vault marked the first stage in the gradual movement toward Gothic architecture, where the rib plays a much more vital structural and visual role.

The other major innovations in Romanesque architecture are found in three types of extended ground plans for the east ends

of churches, the areas reserved for the clergy, the celebration of holy rites, and the veneration of saints and relics. The first two new ground plans, the "radiating" plan and the "stepped" or "staggered" plan, were conceived in what today is France, while the third, sometimes referred to as the "double transept" plan, appeared first in Saxony.

Two explanations may be given for the sudden architectural expansion of churches: the increasing worship of individual saints and relics, and the new practice of having priests say mass every day. A single altar could no longer suffice, and the construction of extra chapels seemed the only sensible solution. The rapid growth of community life and, most important of all, the growing popularity of religious pilgrimages

VI-2. **Principal centers of Romanesque art.**

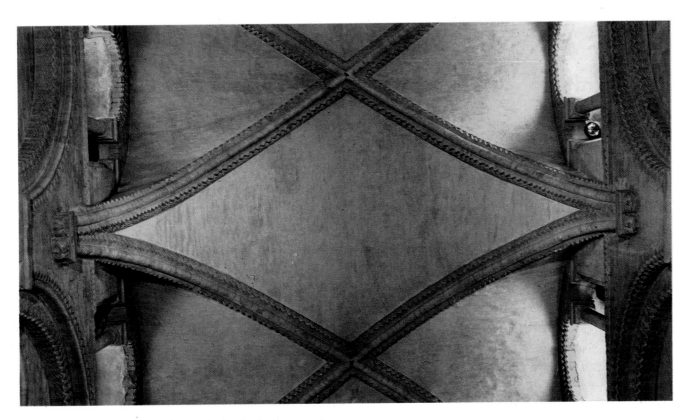

VI-3. **Ribbed vault, Durham Cathedral** (*c.* 1130).

also warranted the building of churches spacious enough to accommodate large crowds. And what helped make this possible were generous financial endowments from both the Church and the nobility.

Saint Martin of Tours, one of the most famous churches in Christendom, is the oldest to have a radiating plan at its east end. Following a fire in 997, it was reconstructed, being consecrated in 1014 and 1020. The church was renowned as the starting point for pilgrimages to Santiago de (Saint James of) compostela, a Spanish shrine revered in the Middle Ages almost as much as any shrine in Jerusalem or Rome. It is said of the Apostle James, brother of John and the patron saint of Spain, that on one of his pilgrimages he journeyed to compostela and thus brought Christianity to Spain. Returning to Judea, he was beheaded by Herod; later, his body was transported to Spain, only to be lost during the Arab invasions, but eventually it was recovered, brought to Compostela, and enshrined. In Spain, the great churches like Santiago de Compostela have been much altered since the Romanesque epoch, yet the remnants of their original structure show beyond doubt that the Spanish imitated the style and building techniques of the French. Spanish Romanesque churches resemble those French ones that studded the pilgrimage routes into Spain, particularly in the eastern provinces, while to the west, Moorish influences can be seen in popular, as opposed to official, architecture.

At Saint Martin of Tours the apse was completely vaulted and the radiating chapels opened off the ambulatory, permitting the congregation to circulate more easily around the sanctuary, with its altars and relics. A similar plan, with minor apses, forming the whole or part of a semicircle, clustered about the main apse, is shown in a ground plan for the Church of Saint Sernin in Toulouse (Plate VI-4); how the radiating plan affects the exterior appearance of a church can be seen in the photograph of the Church of Saint Stephen in Nevers (1063–1097) in Plate VI-5.

The Abbey Church of Cluny in Burgundy, reconstructed under the supervision of Abbot Majeul and consecrated in 981, is the first major monument in which the stepped or staggered layout occurs. The main apse in this type of ground plan is flanked by two or more shorter, subordinate apses. These minor apses flank the main one and act as terminals for the side aisles (see Plate VI-6).

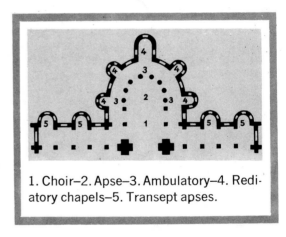

1. Choir—2. Apse—3. Ambulatory—4. Rediatory chapels—5. Transept apses.

VI-4. "Radiating" ground plan for the Church of Saint-Sernin, Toulouse.

The ground plan for the Church of Saint Michael of Hildesheim in Saxony (c. 1000–1003), with two transepts and two apses (see Plate VI-7), is the first known of its kind. The second apse at the west end of the church preempts the customary location of the entrance, which, under this new arrangement, has been shifted to the side of the nave (see Plate VI-8). In northern

VI-5. The Church of Saint Stephen at Nevers (1063–1097).

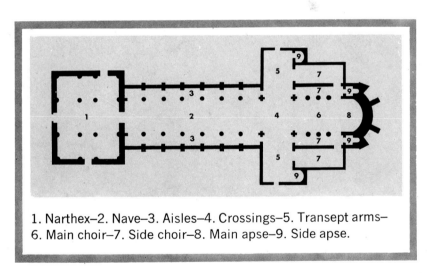

1. Narthex—2. Nave—3. Aisles—4. Crossings—5. Transept arms—6. Main choir—7. Side choir—8. Main apse—9. Side apse.

VI-6. "Stepped" ground plan for the Abbey Church of Cluny.

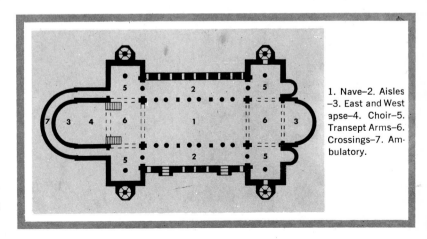

1. Nave—2. Aisles—3. East and West apse—4. Choir—5. Transept Arms—6. Crossings—7. Ambulatory.

VI-7. "Double transept" ground plan for the Church of Saint Michael, Hildesheim.

VI-8. **The Church of Saint Michael, Hildesheim** (*c.* 1000–1003).

VI-9. **Worms Cathedral** (*c.* 1171–1220).

Europe, churches tended to be built to even greater heights than those elsewhere, and the impression of height was further enhanced by the addition of towers and spires such as are seen here. The center of the church was indicated by a great tower at the crossing of the transept and the nave. At Worms (see Plate VI-9) and in numerous other German cathedrals, two smaller towers flank the apse, giving the building something of the aspect of a fortress, a physical and spiritual bastion dominating its surroundings.

On the whole, German architecture tended toward a severe and somewhat heavy concept of form that was derived from classical models and the imperial styles of Charlemagne and Otto the Great. However, with the evolution of the Abbey of Hildesheim and the double transept plan, the Romanesque style gradually took command.

In the north of Europe the most inventive regional architectural school was that of Normandy; the schools of Alsace and Lorraine, together with that of Île-de-France, the Parisian region, remained more faithful to Carolingian traditions. Normandy derives its name from its Viking conquerors, the Norsemen, descendants of the murderous and piratical raiders who had systematically ravaged the coasts of Europe in the centuries preceding the Romanesque period. Settling in the northwestern coastal regions of France sometime about the year 1000, these Norman conquerors originated in this area a school of architecture that was both inventive, as we have said, and influential. The chief characteristics of the style were its uncluttered clarity of wall area, its lack of sculpture, and most importantly, its pursuit of height. Impressive height became increasingly typical of architecture in Normandy and in the neighboring regions where Norman artistic influence was strong.

Of all the monuments in the Romanesque style among the most imposing is the Church of Saint Stephen at Caen. It was erected between the years 1064 and 1077 by the dynamic duke of Normandy, otherwise known as William the Conqueror, who was to invade England successfully two years after construction had gotten under way. The soaring towers, typically Norman, are emphasized by the solid masses of the building's lower zones; its austere roofs are covered with slate (see Plates VI-10 and VI-11).

VI-10. **Church of Saint Stephen at Caen.**

VI-11. **Church of Saint Stephen at Caen (1064–1077).**

VI-12. **Durham Cathedral (1093–1133).**

VI-13. **Interior of Durham Cathedral.**

The arrival of the Normans in England marked a notable change in the artistic trend of the country, although the conquered Anglo-Saxons, upon whose society a foreign aristocracy had now been imposed, were allowed to continue working in their native traditions. The Norman invaders, for their part, continued to devote the greater part of their creative energy to architecture. To ignore the positive and worthwhile achievement of Anglo-Saxon builders during the eleventh and the twelfth centuries would be a mistake; nevertheless it is inescapably true that the Normans shaped the general style of English medieval architecture.

The fine Cathedral of Durham (Plate VI-12) is a Norman building. Begun in 1093, Durham Cathedral is one of the most fascinatingly complex of the Romanesque monuments. New elements in its structure gave rise to a new realm of architectural forms. While the ribbed vault (see Plate VI-13) points the way toward the oncoming

VI-14. **Nave of Ely Cathedral (mid-twelfth century).**

VI-15. **Rochester Castle (1130–1140).**

Gothic style, the massive heaviness of the structure remains solidly Romanesque. The harmonious balance and the serenity of the interior seem to reflect the deepest aspirations of medieval man.

Greater airiness and lightness is found in the Cathedral of Winchester, under construction during the same period as Durham. The more open structure of Winchester lets in light and shows the concern of the architect to relieve the solemnity and oppressiveness of the weighty stone.

This desire for brighter illumination and a dissatisfaction with the sense of weight bearing down upon the worshiper can also be seen in the cathedrals of Norwich and Petersborough, which, like Ely Cathedral (Plate VI-14), were finished in the Gothic period. As in the case of Durham, they suggest the transition from Romanesque to Gothic architecture.

At the same time that the Normans were creating the new cathedrals, abbeys, and churches in England, William the Con-

tangular ground plan, this huge Norman "keep" is further defended at the corners by four great battlemented towers over 130 feet in height.

Stone castles were introduced in Europe in the eleventh century, and from that time on a nobleman's stature could be measured by the thickness and soundness of his walls. Stone also replaced the palisades of wooden stakes previously used for fortifications, moats began to surround great castles, and it seemed that everywhere watchtowers now surveyed the important crossroads of the Romanesque world.

In Italy, various regional styles of architecture developed along their own lines throughout the Romanesque period in Lombardy, Tuscany, and Venice to the north, and in Rome and the island of Sicily to the south.

North Italian abbeys and churches of this time tended to be massive, with long, low, horizontal lines and basically flat facades. Clusters of piers (slender columns) began to take the place of sturdier-looking, single-column arcades, and galleries of stepped arcades appeared frequently as architectural decoration beneath the eaves of churches. Plate VI-16 shows the cloister and the crossing tower of the Abbey of Chiaravalle. From the very earliest times, brick had been used as a basic building material in Lombardy. The brick foundations of this beautiful abbey were built in 1136, and shortly thereafter, the construction of the church began. The fourteenth-century tower, a later addition, is an imitation of Saint Sernin at Toulouse. Another characteristic of Lombard architecture is the clear separation of the structure's parts into simple, blocklike masses of masonry, as can be seen in the eleventh-century Basilica of Sant' Ambrogio in Milan (Plate VI-17).

In Tuscany, many typical Romanesque

VI-16. The Abbey of Chiaravalle (twelfth to fourteenth centuries).

queror and his successors were also carrying out an intensive campaign of fortification. An outstanding example of their style of military architecture is the Castle of Rochester (Plate VI-15), built by the order of William of Corbeuil, Archbishop of Canterbury, between about 1130 and 1140. A massive, thick-walled construction on a rec-

VI-17. The Basilica of Sant' Ambrogio, (eleventh century) Milan.

buildings are sheathed in marble casings; in Florence, geometric patterns were composed with pieces of thin marble veneer, while in Pisa, contrasting bands of light and dark marble were preferred. Florentine architects and sculptors worked with simple forms austerely set in a coherent and clearly defined space, a tendency which did much to revive classical forms. The Church of San Miniato al Monte (Plate VI-18) and the Baptistery of San Giovanni (Plate VI-19), the oldest Romanesque monument in Tuscany, show the absolute clarity and mathematical accuracy with which the decorative marble elements could be organized into lucid, attractive overall designs.

VI-18. The Church of San Miniato al Monte, (*c.* 1140–1150) Florence.

VI-19. The Baptistery of San Giovanni, (eleventh to thirteenth centuries) Florence.

One of the most original and accomplished architects of the Romanesque period was Buscheto, the creator of the supremely handsome and majestic cathedral at Pisa (Plate VI-20). The form of his cathedral is articulated, or given linear emphasis, by the slow and noble rhythm of the arcading. The roots of its style lie in many different cultures, but the final synthesis, the combining of them into an individual whole, is Buscheto's alone, and the unity of style in the cathedral is absolute. Several other architects followed Buscheto in planning parts of the cathedral, among them Diotisalvi and Bonanno, who laid down the main lines of the Baptistery between 1152 and 1278, and also of the campanile, the famous leaning bell tower of Pisa, which was begun in 1173 and eventually completed at the end of the fourteenth century.

Bells for summoning the faithful to church were first mentioned in the sixth century. One or more bells were used by almost every church throughout the Middle Ages, and the size of the bell usually corresponded to the size and importance of the church, as in the case of the great Canterbury Cathedral in England, where twenty-four energetic men were needed to toll a mammoth bell.

Throughout the medieval period, Italy's maritime republic of Venice served as an important commercial and artistic link with the Orient and the Byzantine Empire. In her architecture, Venice consistently demonstrated a style independent of that of her neighbors. The spirit that animated the design of the Basilica of Saint Mark (Plate VI-21), for example, is utterly alien to the architecture of Lombardy. With its superbly luminous interior, Saint Mark's resembles a larger version of San Vitale in Ravenna; the style of the building is clearly derived from that of Byzantine churches

VI-20. The Baptistery, the Cathedral, and the Leaning Tower of Pisa.

VI-21. The Basilica of Saint Mark, (*c.* 1063–1094) Venice.

there and elsewhere and has little in common with true Romanesque. From the illustration of the interior (Plate VI-22), we can form a clearer idea of how Hagia Sophia must have looked during the reign of Justinian (see Plate II-13).

Centers of Romanesque architecture in southern Italy were located at Bari in Apulia and at Palermo in Sicily as well as Rome. In the middle of the eleventh century, the Normans conquered Sicily, bringing about a synthesis of Norman, Byzantine, and Arab styles. The Arab influence had come about because of Sicily's proximity to the Arab world, and it reveals itself in the use of color as a decorative device, in the pointed arches, and in the interlaced or overlapping arcades that were incorporated in the plans for the cathedral at Monreale, begun about 1174 and completed within a decade (see Plate VII-23).

VI-22. **Interior of Saint Mark's, Venice.**

Romanesque Sculpture
and Painting

THE ROMANESQUE PERIOD saw the rebirth of sculpture in the West principally as a form of storytelling and architectural decoration. Rarely treated as an end in itself, Romanesque sculpture is almost always subordinated to the architectural setting, disciplined to fit snugly into it rather than allowed to stand apart. The characteristic qualities revealed in Romanesque sculpture are identical to those suggested by other Romanesque art forms—an almost forbidding sense of religious fervor, a masculine severity and directness, a simple, appealing expressiveness, and the solemnly thrilling gravity of a Gregorian chant or a knight's oath to his lord.

As we have indicated, the political divisions of Europe in the eleventh and the twelfth centuries bore little relation to present national divisions, and when it comes to artistic styles, these tended to follow regional rather than any so-called national lines. Regional styles were frequently determined by the monastic order established in the area and by the presence of trade routes or pilgrimage roads. The stopping places along the pilgrimage routes were marked by spacious and splendid churches where the pilgrims could rest or pass their time meditating upon the carved sculptural decorations. Reliefs and attached statues decorated door jambs and tympanums (the triangular or semicircular areas above portals), facades, windows, baptismal fonts, and the capitals of columns. It has been said that in the Romanesque period a church was like a book to the illiterate: both sculpture and painting were a kind of picture writing.

Bible stories were illustrated everywhere in stone in a lively, blunt, and forceful style. At Vézelay and Autun, sculptors of genius created some of the most appealing representations of Biblical scenes ever carved in any phase of medieval art.

In the region now called France, the most influential school or style was the one originated at the great Abbey Church of Cluny in Burgundy. This abbey diffused a distinct style over a huge area because of its large number of "daughter" or dependent, houses. Each of the most important daughter houses, such as those at Tournus and Autun, in turn headed a minor group within the great Cluniac family.

Airiness and light characterize the great churches dependent upon Cluny; a second distinctive feature is the enormous quantity of sculpture. In Burgundy, sculpture, despite its general subordination in Romanesque art, began to assume an independent life; sometimes its bursting vitality even threatened to dominate the building it surrounded. Decorative rhythms are flowing, and often strange, contorted, and monstrous shapes emerge. Subject matter, too, expresses a new excitement and a desire for colorful narrative. The wide range of pictorial subjects indicates the main currents of medieval intellectual thought: the Last Judgment, the Labors of the Months, the Vices and the Virtues, the Combat of Good against Evil, allegorical representations of the seasons, the four elements, and the signs of the zodiac.

The Last Judgment, a topical holdover from the supposedly calamitous year 1000, appears most frequently, particularly as a theme for tympanums. An example of one of these many representations may be seen in the west tympanum of the Cathedral of Saint Lazarus at Autun (Plate VII-1); it bears the signature of its sculptor, Gislebertus, who is thought to have worked at Autun sometime between the year 1125 and 1135. Here, Christ, draped in intricate pleats and framed in a stone *mandorla,* starkly presides over the Blessed and the Damned. Also attributed to Gislebertus is the famous fragment of a relief from the same cathedral in which Eve, apple in hand and looking as if she were undulating through seaweed, bends over to whisper into Adam's ear (Plate VII-2). This is one of the rare representations of a nude in Romanesque art.

Although the imagination of the Romanesque sculptor turned easily to the monstrous, the fabulous, and the grotesque, the style developed a growing ability to represent contemporary life with unaffected sim-

VII-1. *The Last Judgment,* attributed to Gislebertus, west tympanum of the cathedral at Autun (twelfth century).

VII-2. *The Temptation of Eve,* relief sculpture by Gislebertus. (*c.* 1130).

plicity and realism. In yet another fragment from Autun, showing a praying monk (Plate VII-3), the care that has been taken in reproducing the roughly woven texture of the habit gives us a detailed picture of monastic dress at that time. The Romanesque flair for monsters and demons may strike us today as being both artistically inventive and, at the same time, gruesomely entertaining. But to men of that period, the theatrical and explicit tortures of the damned, such as are demonstrated in *The Last Judgment* at Conques (Plate VII-4), were assumed to be horrifyingly accurate. In this tympanum, traces of paint can still be detected; frequently, brilliant blues, reds, and yellows blared forth from the painted surface of the carved stone, introducing a welcome note into the colorless lives of the peasantry. Cut flowers provided their only other vivid visual pleasure; earlier, during the reign of Charlemagne, peasants had been ordered to wear drab and somber colors so that gentlefolk could be distinguished from them at a glance. During the Romanesque period, even stricter limitations were imposed upon the quality and quantity of material that could be used in their dress. The length and width had always to be the same, and thus, through local laws and customs, standard national costume came into being; like *lederhosen,* the traditional suspended leather shorts still worn in Germany today, these standardized garments, intended to fit anyone, were then handed down from one generation to the next.

The triumph of French Romanesque sculpture, dating from the twelfth century,

is found at Moissac and Souillac in Languedoc (see map in Plate VI-2). The sculptural decoration of the Romanesque doorway at the cloistered Abbey of Souillac (Plate VII-5) closely resembles that of the Church of Sainte-Piene in Moissac (Plate VII-6) in the same bold elongation of the figures, the same dancing rhythms and dramatic gestures. As can be seen from these examples, the new mood was one of agitated movement, bounding vitality, and mystic exultation. Scholars have traced its sources, in part, to Syrian, Armenian, and even Persian influence. Furthermore, it seems certain that at this time a great impetus toward the strange and the exotic was given by crusaders returning from the East. Possibly they influenced artists with their tales of the Orient, and they may have indeed brought tapestries, miniature paintings, or ivories back with them. Some

VII-3. *Praying Monk,* fragment from the cathedral at Autun.

VII-4. *The Last Judgment,* detail from west portal of Sainte-Foy, (eleventh and twelfth centuries) Conques.

VII-5. *Jeremiah,* detail from the doorway of the Abbey Church
at Souillac (1130–1140).

VII-6. Detail from the doorway of the Church
of Sainte-Piene at Moissac (*c.* 1115–1120).

VII-7. Figures of the Apostles, detail from the portal of Saint-Trophime at Arles (*c.* 1125).

VII-8. Juggler, fragment from the portal of Saint-Pierre-le-Pucellier at Bourges (twelfth century).

historians even suggest that European artists may have actually participated in the Crusades and thus gained a firsthand knowledge of the artistic styles of the East. In any case, the range of formal expression was inevitably extended by a stimulating influx of alien ideas and styles. Certainly the haunting figure of Jeremiah at Souillac, with his swirling draperies and wild guru-like beard, represents a drastic departure from the sturdy little dolls standing judgment in the tympanum of the Church of Sainte-Foy at Conques or the solemn saints, clearly influenced by classic Roman models, guarding the portal of Saint-Trophime at Arles (Plate VII-7). The new swirling lines and exaggerated postures reappear later in the splendid stone juggler (Plate VII-8) from the portal of Saint-Pierre-le-Pucellier at Bourges, although the juggler's contorted activity is still forcibly restrained within a tight architectural frame in the strict Romanesque tradition.

Further examples of the subordination of Romanesque sculpture to architectural structure may be seen. A deeply carved hunting scene (Plate VII-9) set in a vineyard decorates a capital from the Church of Saint Magdalen at Vézelay, yet the capital continues to fulfill its structural function as support for an arcade. Carved capitals such as this abound in the Romanesque world, while the following example is a perhaps less common union between sculpture and architecture. Supporting the weight of a column at Modena Cathedral a ferocious stone lion (Plate VII-10) crouches in the act of striking down a heretic. Lions usually represent a vigilant Church in medieval art; they appear once more in Plate VII-11, guarding the base of a *cathedra,* a bishop's throne, from the Church of San Nicola at Bari. (The cathedra, from which "cathedrals" derive their name, was where the bishop sat during solemn feasts of the church.)

The Labors of the Months were used as decorative motifs in Italy, as elsewhere, in Romanesque sculpture. The relief in Plate VII-12, in which a cooper is seen hammering rings around a barrel, illustrates one of these labors and was probably carved by Benedetto Antelami, who in 1178 signed and dated a relief of the deposition of Christ in Parma Cathedral; a detail from that relief in which dice are tossed for Christ's robe appears in Plate VII-13.

Antelami, it appears, traveled north to France several times in his career, and he attempted to transfer to Italian buildings what he had seen there. He was also affected, however, like many of his contem-

VII-9. **Hunting scene, carved capital from the Church of Saint Magdalen, (twelfth century). Vézelay.**

VII-10. **Supporting lion from a column at Modena Cathedral. (1099–1184)**

VII-11. Bishop's throne from the Church of San Nicola at Bari. (*c.* 1098)

VII-12. Relief of one of the Labors of the Months, probably by Benedetto Antelami, from the exterior of the Baptistery of Parma (1190–1200).

poraries, by the strong current of Byzantinism still prevalent in Italy. What is most striking in his work, though, is the growth of dramatic impact. His figures begin to register emotion, not only through movement and gesture, but through facial expression as well. As can be seen in Plate 102, the mourners and the soldiers around the Cross are carefully detailed, revealing an artistic interest in observed reality that was unprecedented in earlier Italian Romanesque sculpture. And Antelami's innovations were to be carried on, for refinements in modeling became greatly advanced as

sculptors gained increasing mastery over the stone they worked with.

In Romanesque painting, as in sculpture, the same strict principle of subordination to the architectural background applied. Fortunately such was the skill of Romanesque artists that time and again they managed to shrug off this limitation. At Tavant, for example, in a wall painting of Christ's descent into Limbo (Plate VII-14), it looks as if the artist had deliberately chosen an inverted trapezoid to frame his work instead of adapting his composition to fit between the two arches of the church.

Undoubtedly by far the most original aspect of the Romanesque style in Spain is contained in the wealth of painting that survives there, especially from the region known as Catalonia. In this area Romanesque painting assumed various forms, appearing most notably as mural decoration in the churches and as illustrations on wooden panels for use as altar pieces. Catalan painting is characterized by its bright colors, flat patterns and simplified shapes, strong outlines, powerful facial expressions, and uncomplicated narrative style. Spanish artists used color to interest the spectator in every portion of the painted area, in accordance with the complex system of color symbolism followed in medieval times. For example, red, the color of blood, was associated with the emotions

VII-13. Detail of the *Deposition of Christ,* by Benetto Antelami, (1178) Cathedral of Parma.

VII-14. *The Descent of Christ into Limbo,* wall painting at the Church at Tavant (twelfth century).

VII-15. *St. Martin and the Beggar,* Spanish Romanesque panel painting (twelfth century).

VII-16. *Saint Giles and the Sick Man,* fragment of a French Romanesque fresco from the Church of Saint-Aignan (twelfth century).

and could symbolize either love or hate; it also served as the Church's official color for martyred saints. Black, on the other hand, the color of the Prince of Darkness, held associations with witchcraft in the Middle Ages and was used to suggest death, mourning, or sickness. Knowing this, one can read the symbolic meanings in a picture of Saint Martin dividing his cloak with a beggar (Plate VII-15). The scene is a detail from an altar painting generally attributed to the Master of Montgrony, an artist who lived in the second half of the twelfth century. The beggar's black rags denote sickness, sadness, and poverty; Saint Martin's red robe proclaims his noble generosity, while his red banner signifies the triumph of love. An interesting comparison can be made between this powerful, direct painting and a more restrained French Romanesque treatment of a similar theme, Saint Giles bestowing his tunic upon a sick man, in

VII-17. *St. Martin and the Beggar,* Spanish Romanesque panel painting (twelfth century).

a twelfth-century fresco from the collegiate church of Saint-Aignan (Plate VII-16). In both can be recognized the typically Romanesque stylistic device of more or less reducing the muscles of the human body to a decorative pattern, but in the French fresco, Saint Giles is dressed in blue, the color of heaven and heavenly love. In yet another Spanish interpretation of Saint Martin and the beggar (Plate VII-17), class distinctions are indicated by the contrasting lengths in tunics; the beggar otherwise looks as warmly dressed as his benefactor.

Spanish Romanesque artists were especially adept at portraying both supernatural happenings and suffering in easily comprehensible terms. In Plate VII-18, the Archangels Raphael and Gabriel are represented in the act of saving a soul; the soul is personified as an innocent child being lifted in a shroud toward paradise, which, in turn, is represented as a red infinity of love. In

VII-18. *The Archangels Raphael and Gabriel Saving a Soul,* Spanish Romanesque panel painting (thirteenth century).

The Martyrdom of Saint Judith and Saint Quirinus (Plate VII-19), the victim's tormentors are dressed in tunics of red, which here symbolizes hate, blood, and fire. Flowerlike flames lick at the pot as the martyrs submit to their painful fate with a childishly simple gesture of resignation. The agony of mourning occupies the artist in a twelfth-century panel (Plate VII-20) taken from the tomb of Sancho Saiz de Carillo at Mahamud. Black predominates in the robes and severely striped tunics of the mourners, and one can almost hear their anguished lamentations as they tear their hair and scratch bloody gashes in their faces in the traditional show of grief; even a baby joins in the hysterical self-mutilation.

Whippings, both administered by others and self-inflicted, were thought to drive out sinfulness in the demon-ridden Middle Ages. Physical suffering, needless to say, was essential to martyrdom, and as the lives of the saints gained increasing importance in religious instruction, scenes of torture and execution became an accepted part of religious art. The Passion, the sufferings of Christ between the night of the Last Supper and His death, and especially Christ's crucifixion were represented much more frequently in the Romanesque period than in the past. To the early Christians, crucifixion had signified a criminal's death, and they disdained the idea of portraying Jesus upon a cross, preferring instead to remember Him as eternally youthful, and in moments of joy. Byzantine and Carolingian artists, in their representations of the Passion, never dreamed of portraying the Lord as a humiliated human being stripped of his clothes and suffering terrible wounds. But the dark anxieties and fearful appre-

VII-19. *The Martyrdom of Saint Judith and Saint Quirinus,* panel painting, detail from an altar.

VII-20. *Group of Mourners,* Spanish Romanesque panel painting (twelfth century) Museum of Catalan Art, Barcelona.

VII-21. **Crucifix from the Church of Saint George, (eleventh to twelfth centuries) Milbertshofen.**

hensions of the Middle Ages led to an uneasy atmosphere of morbidity and guilt that seeped grimly into every area of life, and art was no exception. In this way we find a new emphasis upon the suffering of Christ on the cross; artistically, the subject allowed great scope, for the central drama of the Christian faith could be interpreted with the maximum of passion and religious intensity. Examples may be seen in the eleventh- or twelfth-century German crucifix in Plate VII-21 and in two Italian depositions of Christ, one an extremely moving wooden sculpture from Pescia (Plate VII-22), the

VII-22. *The Deposition of Christ,* Italian Romanesque sculpture from the Church of Sant' Antinio at Pescia (thirteenth century).

VII-23. *The Deposition of Christ,* detail of a fresco from the Cathedral at Aquileia (1150–1220?).

other a mural (Plate VII-23) into which the painter has projected so much tragedy that the bonds of Byzantine conventions, here at least, seem to have been finally snapped.

The twelfth century saw a triumphant revival of the art of mosaic in Venice, Sicily, Constantinople, and Greece. In the East, the official central theme in standard Byzantine church decoration was the transformation of Christ into God. This decorative theme was considered so important and was to be realized according to such strict specifications that the building became no more than a frame around it. On the upper walls and on the lower regions of the ceiling area appeared images of saints; higher on the ceiling were scenes from the life of Christ; and in the dome above the apse, a group of the Virgin and Child (in art terminology, as few as two figures may constitute a group). The central dome, the focal point of a Byzantine church, was devoted to a figure of Christ as God Almighty, the "Pantocrator." The religious hierarchy of these zones was absolute: the most holy image of Christ must appear nearest heaven, the Virgin and Child and the scenes from the life of Christ in the second level, and nearest the congregation (earth) a row of saints.

At the Cathedral of Monreale in Sicily (Plate VII-24), one sees a direct adaptation of this Byzantine hierarchy. But in the Palatine Chapel, dedicated to Saint Peter and standing within the remains of the royal palace at Palermo, one finds a surprising mosaic (Plate VII-25) in which classical centaurs are depicted along with leopards and peacocks. Actually the scene is meant to portray evil, man divided within himself, immortality, and the "all-seeing" God. Here the peacock, which we have met before as a Christian symbol, signifies the last two

VII-24. **East end of the Monreale Cathedral, (1174–1184) Sicily.**

VII-25. **Mosaic from the Palatine Chapel at Palermo (1132–1143).**

VII-26. *The Agony in the Garden,* mosaic from the Basilica of Saint Mark in Venice (first half of thirteenth century).

of these subjects; the centaur represents brutal passions, heresy, and man torn between good and evil; and the leopard represents cruelty, the Antichrist, and the Devil—a host of evils.

The brilliant mosaics in the Basilica of Saint Mark in Venice cover a range of familiar subjects, such as Noah and the Ark, and the Agony in the Garden (see Plate VII-26), as well as less familiar religious episodes. Created during the first half of the thirteenth century, these mosaics, in the view of some scholars, represent the work of Byzantine artists. They employ an interesting narrative device that became typical of pictorial art in the oncoming Gothic period: the same figures reappear within a single picture space in the course of a particular story. Christ, for example, is seen both discovering the sleeping Apostles and addressing them in *The Agony in the Garden.* Another narrative device in these mosaics is the inscription of Latin text above the figures, to further clarify the story.

The bringing of the body of Saint Mark to Venice is the subject of the superb mosaic in Plate VII-27. Mark is the patron saint of Venice, because, according to legend, while he was on a mission in the Adriatic, his boat was swept by a violent storm into the islands and lagoons along the northeastern Italian coast, where Venice stands today. An angel suddenly appeared to Mark, declaring, "On this site, a great city will arise in your honor." Mark was killed in Alexandria a dozen years later and buried there, but several centuries after his martyrdom, Venetian sailors stole his body and brought it back to their city. In the Venetian mosaic, the soul of Saint Mark, appearing over his corpse and beneath his name, "S Marcu," directs the deliverers of his dead body to the port of Venice. The soul of Mark is shown wearing the robes of the clergy and with a tonsure, a shaved area at the top of the head. (The custom of shaving the head this way had been adopted by early monastic orders and clergy as a reminder of the perfect life, a remembrance of Christ's crown of thorns, and a symbolic rejection of the fleeting things pertaining to earthly life.)

The Byzantine style sometimes insinuated itself even into French Romanesque art. The carved and painted wooden group in Plate VII-28, in which the Virgin sits upright on an arcaded throne and holds the Christ Child before the faithful so that He may be adored, is highly derivative of similar Byzantine models. On the other hand, a Virgin and Child (Plate VII-29) from the great bronze doors of the Cathedral of Saint Michael at Hildesheim that were cast about the year 1015, in Germany ranking among the finest achievements of Romanesque bronze workers, radiates a wonderful tenderness and natural grace foreign to the Byzantine tradition.

As for the crafts, or "minor arts," they flourished in the eleventh century. Monks and laymen busied themselves as goldsmiths; jewelers; ivory carvers; enamel, glass, and ceramic workers; carpet and silk weavers; tapestry and lace makers; saddlers; engravers; carpenters; and the like. The first tailors' guilds were founded at this time, and new textile industries boomed in France, Germany, and Flanders. As the first Crusade got under way, monastic orders and schools expanded and new towns and markets sprang up. National languages developed more fully, economies improved, and private individuals began increasingly to patronize artisans and craftsmen. As a consequence of the bustling activity in the minor arts, thousands upon thousands of beautiful objects were created; a few examples appear in Plate VII-30 through VII-

VII-28. *Madonna and Child*, painted wooden sculpture from the Auvergne region of France (second half of twelfth century).

VII-29. *Madonna and Child*, detail from the bronze doors of the Cathedral of Saint Michael at Hildesheim (c. 1015).

VII-27. *The Bringing of the Body of Saint Mark to Venice*, mosaic from the Basilica of Saint Mark in Venice.

VII-32. Italian Romanesque book cover in raised gilt copper with semiprecious stones and colored enamels (eleventh century).

VII-30. Flabellum in gilt bronze set with figured crystals and semiprecious stones, German Romanesque (1130–1140).

VII-31. German Romanesque book cover in gilt copper decorated with silver (end of twelfth century).

VII-33. French Romanesque book cover in copper gilt, ivory, and gems (eleventh century).

VII-34. **The Gloucester Candlestick Anglo-Norman metalwork in gilt bronze (*c.* 1109–1113).**

34. The magnificent flabellum, or fan, in Plate VII-30, of gilt bronze set with engraved crystal and semiprecious stones, was used in the Middle Ages as a ceremonial fly whisk to protect the consecrated host during mass. The three lavish book covers in Plates VII-31, VII-32, and VII-33 show the varying styles of Germany, Italy, and France, respectively. And the Gloucester Candlestick (Plate VII-34), the crowning glory of the richly productive bronze workshops of England that flourished in the later Romanesque period, is a masterpiece of the goldsmith's art, mingling Norman, Anglo-Saxon, and Irish decorative elements.

At Winchester, in England, there came into being one of the greatest schools of manuscript painting of the entire Middle Ages. The art of decorating books continued to flourish in that country despite the Norman conquest in 1066; the School of Winchester itself was productive between the tenth and the twelfth centuries. No other manuscript illuminators could match the imaginative invention of the Winchester artists.

A distinct type of foliate, or leafy, decoration and the use of multicolored interlacing designs, the kind usually borrowed today in imitation of medieval motifs, are the unmistakable characteristics of the Winchester School. Both color and line vibrate with a new excitement, and the relationship between text and miniature painting is so close that they often seem to jostle one another on the page. Also notable is a more abstract stylization of human forms, as may be seen in a painted page (Plate VII-35) from the Psalter of Henry of Blois, dating from the middle of the twelfth century, in which an angel locks the gates of hell. The colorful illuminated

VII-35. *The Jaws of Hell Fastened by an Angel,* Winchester School of illumination (twelfth century).

VII-36. Illuminated initial *D* from the Winchester Bible (twelfth century).

initial *D* (Plate VII-36), containing a scene of the Angel of Death striking down the nation of Israel, dates from the same period.

The Bayeux tapestries, commemorating William the Conqueror's triumph over England's Edward the Confessor and his successor King Harold, constitute one of the major artistic delights of the Romanesque period. According to legend, these fascinating embroideries, in which over sixty separate episodes from William's invasion are recorded, were the work of William's Queen Matilda. But it is now known that the narrative tapestries were ordered in England by William's brother, Bishop Odo, for his cathedral of Bayeux. They have survived thanks to the meticulous care and attention given to church property; it is more than likely that many similar tapestries, now lost, once decorated the chilly stone walls of the nobility's castles.

The Bayeux tapestries reflect the joy that artists of the late Romanesque period took in narrative detail; they are also interesting for their rambling, espisodic style of storytelling, a departure from Romanesque unity and a step toward the Gothic love of pictorial and poetic cycles. In Plate VII-37, a battle and surrender scene is depicted with remarkable expressiveness. To the left, the Anglo-Saxons strive valiantly to stave off the enemy; beneath them, two Norman soldiers set fire to their battle tower; and at the right we see a glum, defeated duke relinquishing to William the keys of the city, held dangling from the end of a spear. The tapestries are immensely entertaining, but beneath the spellbinding narration lies a foundation of moving simplicity and unself-conscious honesty, a foundation on which the whole imposing structure of Romanesque art had been based.

VII-37. **Detail from the Bayeaux tapestries (eleventh century).**

DINA NTES ETI

The Gothic Period: France

TODAY THE TERM *Gothic* is normally used to identify a style of art, especially in the area of architecture, that originated and developed in northern Europe, characterizing a period of roughly two centuries, from approximately the middle of the twelfth century until the advent of the Italian Renaissance. The Gothic style managed to survive the revolutionary Italian movement, however, and persisted in many European localities for at least another 150 years. Originally the term *Gothic* had been coined by critics in the sixteenth and seventeenth centuries to apply to all medieval art prior to the Renaissance; the word was meant to suggest something barbarian (it means, literally, "of the Goths"), an inelegant period of artistic production. A revival of interest in the period was seen in the eighteenth century, and the term, stripped of its negative connotations, was adopted by enthusiasts of medieval or "Gothic" art. When in the nineteenth century the "Romanesque" period became designated as such, the Gothic age had its early era arbitrarily chopped off, leaving scholars with the vaguely applicable date of 1140, when the choir of Saint Denis was begun, as a starting point from which to proceed in documenting the evolution of the Gothic style.

The dominant mood of the Romanesque period had been set by the solemnity of its massive, cavelike cathedrals. With the appearance of the Gothic style, a bright light, quite literally, was cast upon religious architecture, dissolving the austere shadows of the past.

In twelfth-century France, the artistic forms developed during the Romanesque period were briskly carried toward a different ideal by this Gothic style. Credit for the abrupt shift in artistic currents is traditionally given to the worldly and ambitious Suger (1081–1151), Abbot of Saint Denis, near Paris. Suger personified many of the qualities characteristic of the Gothic age, and his attitude helps us understand more fully the fundamental differences between the Romanesque and the Gothic spirits. The key to his eventually triumphant philosophy can be found in a line from one of his lengthy treatises, *De Administratione:* "It is only through symbols of beauty that our poor spirits can raise themselves from things temporal to things eternal."

Suger's ideals conflicted sharply with those of Bernard, Abbot of Clairvaux (1091–1153), whose devotion to work and prayer and whose emphatic denial of the worth of the physical senses eventually led to his sainthood. Saint Bernard championed the simple life, and he exerted an unshakable influence over a vast network of more than 350 European Cistercian monasteries before his death.

Saint Bernard demanded self-denial and condemned riches and decoration in churches as ungodly distractions to the mind bent on meditation. Suger, on the contrary, believed that the way toward God could be discovered through worldly experience. Physical beauty, he felt, could reflect some part of the glory of creation. Gothic art can to some extent be explained by this belief, that in enriching every object and building, man is at the same time glorifying God.

The ninth-century scholar John Scotus Erigena had earlier written that "we understand a piece of wood or stone only when we see God in it." Throughout the Medieval period men subscribed to this statement, for in medieval thought there was no room for material beauty as an end in itself. Life represented merely a brief phase in the journey of the spirit. Meditation and prayer took unquestioned precedence over physical activity of any sort, and as a steady occupation, manual labor, in particular, was looked upon with scorn as having little or no bearing on the ideally spiritual life. Spiritual or theological meaning was thus thought to be the only true merit of religious art, never its style or the skill or originality of its particular creator.

A romantic myth has been handed down from the Middle Ages to the effect that the anonymity of individual artists sprang from an overwhelming impulse of selflessness and communal religious zeal. This is not true. Medieval artists and artisans bore about the same public image as plumbers do today; that contemporary authors spend little time in the literary appreciation of sanitary facilities does not seem strange to us; similarly, it rarely occurred to educated men to document or explain the course of art until the Renaissance, when at last the activities of European artists were treated as subjects worthy of constant historical attention.

For these reasons, no one knows who actually designed the original architectural plan for Suger's reconstruction of the Church of Saint Denis (Plate VIII-1), the church of the royal family that was dedicated to the patron saint of France and that served as the burial place of kings until the French Revolution. Suger recorded much detailed information concerning the progress of this great project, in which three of the major features of Gothic architecture

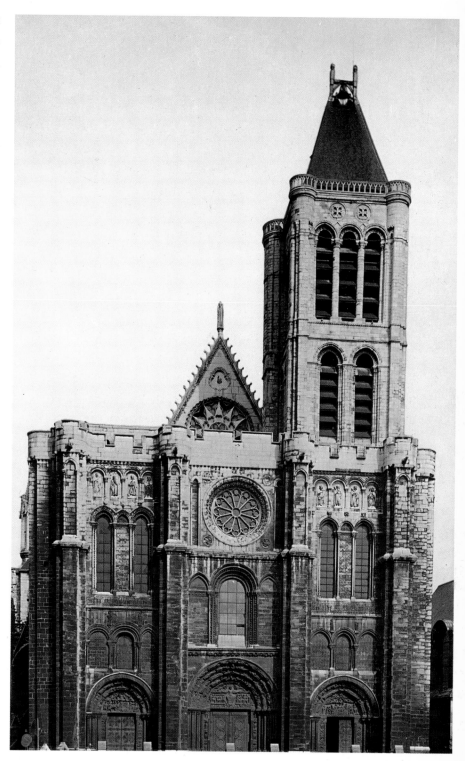

VIII-1. The Abbey of Saint Denis, French Gothic (begun in 1140).

VIII-2. **Nave of the Abbey of Saint Denis.**

The new choir of Saint Denis, begun in 1140 and finished within a period of four years, unquestionably owes a great deal of its inspiration to Suger's intellect and love of sumptuous decoration, and although many of the particular characteristics of Saint Denis already existed in various Norman and Burgundian churches, their combination in one building produces an effect of startling originality (see Plate VIII-2). The foundations of the Gothic style were laid at Saint Denis with the incorporation of the pointed arch, the ribbed vault, and the flying buttress (Plates VIII-3–VIII-4); the pointed arch, even more than the tall blazing windows of jewel-covered glass or the fantastic prickly spires, would become the most conspicuous characteristic in Gothic architecture.

The structural innovations in Gothic architecture, based upon the three newly wed features, permitted architects, among other things, to vary the radius of an arch, within certain limits, and to resolve the problem of lighting a cathedral. The Gothic cathedral, with its complex network of interacting forces, came close to eliminating the heavy wall masses of earlier architecture. As the walls became no longer so vital to the support of the vaults, whose weight was now carried to fixed points on buttresses, they could be pierced by soaring windows. Flying buttresses made it possible to increase the height of the vaults and consequently of the windows, by carrying the stress away from the walls. Light and space were henceforth allowed to become as important as the tense filigree of stone that contained them.

In the Île-de France, in the areas around Paris as far as the Loire, and throughout the royal domain, the new ideas first put into practice at Saint Denis spread rapidly. The successive stages in the evolution of Gothic

appear together for the first time, but he never once mentioned the name of the architect or architects responsible for the plan.

Suger was a brilliant statesman and gave counsel to two kings of France—Louis the Sixth, known as Louis the Fat, and his son, Louis the Young, the first husband of Eleanor of Aquitaine. Two great desires drove Suger on—he sought to strengthen the crown of France and to enrich his own abbey. He managed to combine these two ambitions, for by making Saint Denis more glorious, he inevitably drew attention to the wealth and the authority of the king.

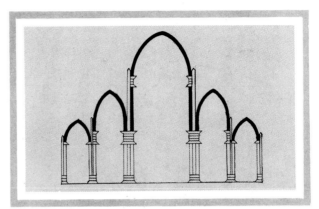

VIII-4. Diagram of pointed arches.

VIII-4. Structure of a Gothic vault.

VIII-3. Rib vaults at Meaux Cathedral (twelfth to fifteenth centuries).

VIII-4. Diagram of flying buttresses.

VIII-5. **Notre Dame, Paris (1160–1250)**

architecture can be followed in the many cathedrals that sprang up in this region. Built within only a few years of each other—Noyon in about 1150, Laon about 1155, Notre Dame in Paris about 1160, and Chartres (in its rebuilt form about 1194) (see Plates VIII-5–VIII-8)—these cathedrals each contributed something to a formula that was to be used, with various modifications, for three hundred years to come. For example, the wall area on either side of the nave, referred to as the elevation, had customarily been divided into three stories or zones: from the ground upward rose the arcade, then came the gallery,

and finally there was the clerestory with its modest windows. At Noyon, however, an extra story began to appear for the first time, breaking up the wall surface still further into four different zones (see similar plan in Plate VIII-9, the nave of Laon Cathedral).

The creative fervor of the Gothic architects continued unabated; in each successive church something new appeared and some part of the older tradition was renewed or cast aside. At Chartres, rebuilt after a fire in 1194, the complete unity of interior space is achieved. From the bases of the piers (stone supports) to the keystones (the

VIII-6. Chartres Cathedral (1195–1260).

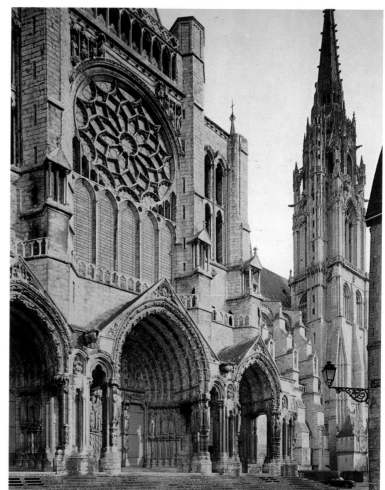

VIII-7. Facade of Laon Cathedral (1180–1220).

VIII-8. Laon Cathedral (1180–1220).

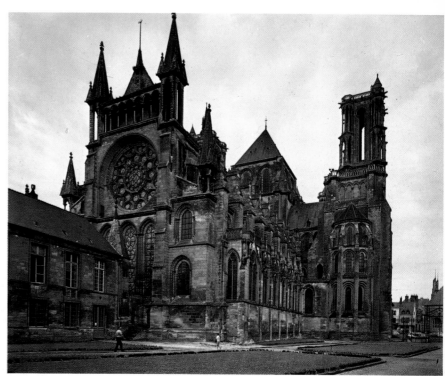

VIII-9. **The nave of Laon Cathedral.**

the area of sculpture. The transept facades, for example, contain an important series of early Gothic figures. Before we discuss the sculpture of Chartres in detail, however, let us first look at the background of Gothic sculpture.

The evolution of sculpture from the Romanesque into the Gothic style occurred rather more slowly than did that of architecture. The most obvious difference between Romanesque and Gothic sculpture can be seen in the increasingly natural human, animal, and plant forms created by Gothic artists. The stark austerity and rigid symbolism of Romanesque sculpture gave way to a new awareness of the natural world; this transition represents the relatively liberal Gothic trend of thought, known as nominalism, a branch of Scholasticism. Prior to the Gothic period, it had been believed that all scientific knowledge had been revealed by the Scriptures. The Church had officially interpreted the Bible and had allowed no arguments to be raised; now, a questioning mood could be sensed. People began to wonder about life in this world as well as in the hereafter, if only on a limited scale, and men such as Saint Francis (1182–1226), appalled by the gulf between the rich and the poor, sympathetically took the vow of poverty in their devotion to God and mankind. The nominalists recalled the words of Saint Thomas, "God enjoys all things, for each accords with his essence," claiming that every particular thing had a place in the universe and a share in being, and the radical Franciscan concept of brotherhood now demanded that love be shown to all living creatures. Art could not help but profit by this welcome sunshine of spiritual freedom, and it responded by blossoming into graceful new forms.

highest meeting point of the slender vault ribs), each single part and detail is related to the others, and all are combined into a magnificent whole. The clerestory windows are no longer small, as they had been in Romanesque churches, and they fill the width of each bay. The shafts of the main piers now sweep up through the gallery and the clerestory to the ribs of the vaults without interruption, creating a thrusting vertical movement (see Plate VIII-10). From the great piers and clustered shafts to the vaults far above, the continuous movement of line and form, as if charged by some electric energy, irresistibly draws the spectator's eye heavenward.

On its exterior, too, Chartres made its contributions to Gothic art, particularly in

It must be understood that it is the new treatment of sculpture, rather than any drastic change in subject matter or function, that shows most clearly the development of the Gothic sculptural style. Only gradually did sculpture grow independent of its architectural framework to the point that it was able to make a dramatic impact in its own right.

The evolution of Gothic sculpture, which attained maturity as an artistic style toward the end of the twelfth century and during the first decades of the thirteenth century, began in all probability at the Abbey of Saint Denis. Unfortunately, little now remains of the sculptural decoration that once adorned this historic building. The earliest surviving examples are found at Chartres and at Senlis, and already these are much less rigid in their style than any comparable church sculpture of the Romanesque epoch.

The triple Royal Portal of Chartres Cathedral has three typanums that contain, from left to right, these principal scenes: *The Ascension; Christ of the Apocalypse* (Plate VIII-11), with the four symbols of the Evangelists so familiar from Romanesque

VIII-10. **Chartres, (mid-twelfth century).**

VIII-11. *Christ of the Apocalypse,* detail from the Royal Portal at Chartres.

art; and *The Mystery of the Incarnation.* Scenes such as the middle one here, showing Christ of the Apocalypse, or "Christ in Glory," were to become the usual theme for the Gothic tympanum. On the door jambs of the Royal Portal appear a procession of prophets and other figures from the Old Testament. The figures (Plate VIII-12) are elongated to an extreme degree, a typically Gothic stylization, and their draperies are indicated by an almost flat decorative pattern of finely chiseled parallel lines. The statues here are still closely bound to the wall surface and their function as columns remains obvious, but now the adventurous impulse of the sculptor has given these celebrated figures a striking and expressive physical individuality. The figure of Christ, in particular, reveals a new sensitivity to character; the serene humanity of His expression has never even been approached in Romanesque art.

In comparison with the mid-twelfth-century sculpture that decorates the Royal Portal, the sculpture elsewhere at Chartres, from workshops of the early thirteenth century, demonstrates a much firmer grasp of structural principles. Although the

VIII-12. Figures from the Royal Portal at Chartres.

VIII-13. *The Blessing Christ,* detail from the central door of the south portal of Chartres (early thirteenth century).

VIII-14. Figures from the south portal of Chartres.

VIII-15. *The Last Judgment,* portal of Notre Dame, (*c.* 1220) Paris.

treatment of the drapery is still stiffly formalized, a more realistic approach to proportions is evident. The finest work of this second period of sculpture in the Chartres tradition is the profoundly compassionate figure of the blessing Christ (Plate VIII-13). In the tympanum of the north door, where the life of the Virgin is represented, there appears a balanced composition of symmetrically arranged figures. The actual depth of the sculptural relief work has grown considerably, and the figures, like those seen in a detail from the south portal in Plate VIII-14, are now placed in front of their columns without the customary architectural canopies above their heads to confine them.

The sculpture on the doors of Notre Dame in Paris dates from the beginning of the thirteenth century. The scenes possess a grave but tranquil depth of feeling; they are more in harmony with the world of natural appearances than were previous sculptural scenes; and the figures stand out in finely proportioned attitudes. In the *Last Judgment* portal (*c.* 1220, Plate VIII-15), the scene, as always, is dominated by the figure of Christ the Judge, flanked by the souls of the elect on one side and by the souls of the damned on the other.

Whereas Romanesque sculptors preferred to portray Christ surrounded by the four symbols of the Evangelists, in the Gothic period sculptors preferred a different composition. Christ as the Heavenly Judge formed the psychological and compositional core of their scenes, and subordinate to Him were the Virgin, John the Baptist, and angels bearing the instruments of the Passion. The portal shown in Plate VIII-16, consecrated to the Virgin, illustrates the growing cult of the Mother of God, for the Virgin and her life provided a tenderly moving theme that appealed greatly to Gothic craftsmen. (The statue of the Virgin and Child is a nineteenth-century restoration.) The Madonna in Plate VIII-17, dating from the first half of the fourteenth century and

VIII-17. **Madonna, school of Île-de-France, (fourteenth century).**

VIII-16. **Portal consecrated to the Virgin at Notre Dame, (*c.* 1210–1220) Paris.**

VIII-18. *The Last Judgment,* (fourteenth century) from the tympanum of the central portal of Saint-Étienne Cathedral, Bourges.

still bearing traces of paint, shows again the masterful development of this theme in French Gothic sculpture.

The scene of the Last Judgment (Plate VIII-18) in the tympanum of the central portal of Saint-Étienne Cathedral at Bourges is typically divided into three zones. In the lowest register, the dead arise from their tombs with apprehensive excitement at the blare of the last trumpet. In the central register, individual souls are weighed and separated by the Archangel Michael; the condemned are dragged off by demons toward hell, while the blessed ascend toward paradise. In the topmost register, Christ displays the wounds He suffered for the redemption of humanity. The sculptor's mastery of anatomy is shown to particular advantage in the athletic postures of the souls arising from their tombs.

The Cathedral of Rheims was built between about 1215 and 1240. The sculptural scheme of this cathedral is one of the most fascinating and artistically mature of all such Gothic works, not only in France but throughout western Europe. The influences of classical Greece and Rome can be immediately detected in the draperies and the postures of the very convincing human figures. The north transept doorway, dedicated to Saint Calixtus, appears in Plate VIII-19.

VIII-19. **North transept doorway, dedicated to Saint Calixtus,** (*c.* 1215–1240) Rheims Cathedral.

Numerous important architects are known to have worked at Rheims, among them Jean d'Orbais, Jean Le Loup, Gaucher de Rheims, and Bernard de Soissons. These four seem in general to have directed both architecture and sculpture during the time they spent as masters of the works. In the twelfth and the thirteenth centuries, the construction of large churches and cathedrals was directed by two masters—the *magister lapidum,* the master mason or architect, and the *magister operis,* literally the "master of the works," whose responsibilities were more or less the same as those of a modern-day contractor. The *magister operis* hired the workers and bought all the necessary materials; the *magister lapidum* designed and supervised the plans and coordinated the workers' activities. The artisans and workers at each project would all belong to a cooperative organization known, in English, as a masons' lodge. Sometimes during the Gothic period, when the construction of a cathedral might take decades or even centuries, a lodge might remain at the same location for generation after generation. Upon the completion of a project, it was not uncommon for a lodge to move off in a body under the leadership of the master architect and set up an atelier, or workshop, at another site. In this way architectural and artistic ideas were spread from one end to the other of Europe's "central corridor," that network of major trade routes crisscrossing from London to Bologna, in the north of Italy, and eventually to Prague.

The speed with which a cathedral was constructed inevitably depended upon the availability of money; when we read of a cathedral having taken centuries to complete, periodic lack of funds can always be found at the root of the delay.

The enormous expenses incurred in the course of building a cathedral were defrayed in a variety of ways. In the first place, cathedrals were commissioned by townspeople and their bishops; the rise of the bourgeoisie, or middle class, during the Gothic period meant the creation of a monied segment of society that could be called upon for generous contributions. And the men of the bourgeoisie were only too happy to help; cathedrals not only bolstered civic pride but also led to lucrative business and trade. Pilgrims spent freely, and foreign traders were inclined to do business in towns where they might meet and deal with others of their kind who might be passing through on trading trips or pilgrimages of their own. Naturally both the bishops and the nobility also contributed toward the building of cathedrals, and local societies were formed to raise funds. Holy relics were toured through the countryside in an effort to gather contributions; indulgences and perpetual prayers were sold to benefactors; collection boxes were prominently displayed; and revenues from local monasteries were diverted to meet the expenses of constructing cathedrals.

The pride taken by a community in its cathedral bordered on fanaticism; everyone wished to participate in some phase of its creation, and it was to this end that the "cult of the cart" came into being. Roped together like beasts of burden, grunting and heaving under the tremendous strain, devoted teams of volunteer workers joined together to drag tons of building materials up the customary incline to the cathedral's construction site. Side by side could be counted artists, butchers, money changers, shoemakers, armorers, skinners, pharmacists, youths of the nobility, weavers, shopkeepers, barbers, tavern keepers, actors, and others too numerous to mention. They are all given due credit at Chartres, where they have been immortalized in the famous stained glass of the cathedral; over four thousand figures have been counted in the windows there.

Such stained glass represents the outstanding achievement of northern Gothic painting. With the emergence of the rib vault whose weight was borne by tall and slender piers, the walls of traditional churches, as we have mentioned, no longer had to be constructed of solid masses of stone and instead could be opened up, thereby allowing the sun to pour through the vast and dazzling new colored windows. In this way narrative illustration in northern European Gothic churches was almost completely transferred from the wall surface into the glass itself. This presented a new field for artistic expression, unexplored until the Gothic period seized the opportunity.

The Byzantines had been the first to experiment with stained-glass windows, but by 1100 the French had developed the concept into one of the most distinctive forms of Western medieval art. Among the first important artistic centers where the new potential of stained glass was fully explored were the abbey workshops of Saint Denis. Tragically, however, almost all the stained glass of St. Denis has been destroyed.

The largest quantity of Gothic stained glass to be found in its original setting remains at Chartres; it was from Chartres that the new technique would be diffused throughout France, England, and Germany. Its influence also extended to Italy, but here, mural painting retained its preeminence.

Two methods could be used in making colored glass: the "pot metal" technique called for the addition of metallic oxides to molten glass so that it became colored throughout; the "flashed" technique, a somewhat later development, fused thin sheets of colored glass to ordinary ones. Subtle regulation of temperatures produced a variety of shades in the pot metal technique; ruby red was customarily achieved by flashing.

The window designs were often in the form of geometric shapes, one of the most distinctive being the round window, seen frequently set by itself in the wall of a Gothic cathedral and called a rose window (see facade of Chartres Cathedral in Plate VIII-6). Throughout the thirteenth century, the period of highest accomplishment in glass painting, compositions were first designed in large "cartoons" and transferred to the small individual pieces of glass, which were then set into a lead framework. Details were painted on the colored glass in dull enamel, and then were permanently fused to the surface by a further heating process. In the later Middle Ages, a technique known as *grisaille* grew up; enamel drawings were executed on plain glass, which was then given a silvery yellow finish. This new style was seen more frequently as the thirteenth century progressed. Also, the metal framework increasingly became a broadly spaced iron grid, thereby reducing the mosaic-like quality of the early stained glass and giving the design a more unified aspect.

At Chartres, rich, deep, clear color and predominating reds and blues are hallmarks of the stained glass. Another characteristic of the Chartres style is that the window fields, or areas, are composed with elegant simplicity into such geometric shapes as circles, squares, quatrefoils (literally "four-leafed" shapes), and curved forms. An example of the Chartres stained glass, showing scenes from the life of the Virgin (Chartres was dedicated to the Virgin), can be seen in Plate VIII-20. Plates VIII-21, VIII-22 show windows in which quatrefoils domi-

VIII-20. Scenes from the life of the Virgin, French Gothic stained glass (mid-thirteenth century) Chartres.

VIII-22. Stained-glass window, (twelfth and thirteenth centuries) Chartres.

VIII-21. *Notre Dame de la Belle Verrière* and stained-glass window with quatrefoils, (twelfth and thirteenth centuries) Chartres.

nate the design and also the famous *Notre Dame de la Belle Verrière* (Our Lady of the Beautiful Stained-Glass Window), which was inserted at a later date in the left-hand twelfth century window frame.

The fascinating reproductions in Plate VIII-23 show artisans at work; from left to right appear masons, stonecutters, and sculptors. The particularly memorable expression on the face of a sculptor appraising his work speaks volumes for the profes-

VIII-24. Scene from the *Song of Roland,* stained-glass window, (thirteenth century) Chartres.

VIII-23. Masons, stonecutters, and sculptors from a stained-glass window, (thirteenth century) Chartres. (*pages 112–113*)

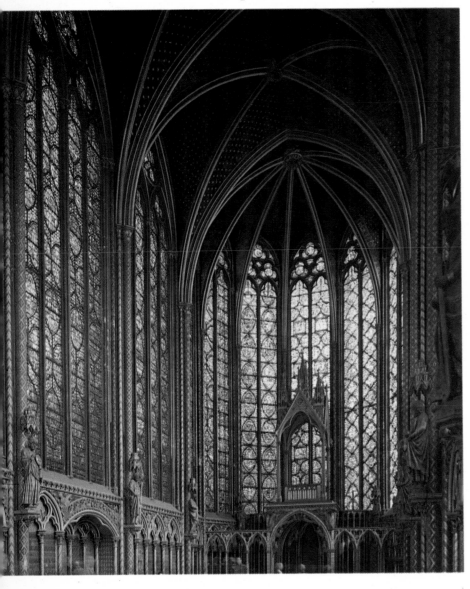

sional creative spirit. Another pictorial theme in the Chartres windows was drawn from the life of Charlemagne as it had been romanticized in the great epic poems of France such as the *Song of Roland*. In Plate VIII-24, Roland is shown trying to smash his sacred and beloved sword, Durandel, so that it may not fall into the hands of the heathen enemy.

The stained-glass compositions of Chartres, with their new decorative motifs, were imitated before long by numerous other French Gothic cathedrals, among them Sens, Bourges, and Rouen. Meanwhile, sometime about the middle of the thirteenth century, another great center of the craft developed in Paris. Part of the series of fifteen magnificent windows erected in 1243 and 1248 in the Sainte-Chapelle in Paris is shown in Plate VIII-25. The slender stone framework of this palace chapel built by Saint Louis, Louis IX, the only French king to become a saint, is completely encrusted with decorative painting and gilding; the huge windows mark a great advance in the transformation of the Gothic wall into a shimmering membrane of glass.

In the area of manuscript illumination, France was to experience a brief interlude of stagnation in the second half of the twelfth century, perhaps as a result of the strict discipline imposed by Saint Bernard's Cistercian orders. However, this period soon passed, and the influence of Abbot Suger and the stimulus of royal patronage contributed considerably to the search for new directions in the arts. The center of the new movement in illumination was Paris. Here the university was being formed into an organized body, and one of the logical results was an increased demand for parchment books.

The use of paper for books did not really become widespread until the fourteenth century. Known in Sicily from 1145, paper, a Chinese invention, had first been brought by the Tartars to the Arabs, who then introduced it to Sicily and Spain. Among the nobility, the possession of exquisitely decorated devotional books was to become a symbol of rank and wealth.

The new style of manuscript illumination bore strong similarities to the enamels and highly finished metalwork of the period (see Plates VIII-26 and VIII-27), and stained glass probably played its part in influencing

VIII-26. *The Resurrection of the Dead,* French Gothic enameled metalwork plaque (mid-thirteenth century).

VIII-28. *Dream of Jacob,* miniature from the Psalter of Saint Louis (*c.* 1253).

VIII-27. School of Limoges reliquary in gold, enamel, and semiprecious stones (early thirteenth century).

the page layout and choice of colors. But the illuminators progressively evolved an unmistakable style of their own. We can see this style in the considerable number of illuminated manuscripts, ordered specifically for members of the royal family or for members of the inner circle of the court, that have survived to this day. These include books of the psalms, evangelistaries, short collections of personal prayers, and illustrated Bibles with accompanying commentaries.

These magnificently decorated manuscripts provided a fitting accompaniment for the glorious stained glass and soaring architecture of the Sainte-Chapelle, where members of the French royal family usually worshipped. The elaborate motifs of the manuscripts tended to imitate the architecture of the Sainte-Chapelle, while the figure style resembled that seen in the work of the royal glass painters. Examples are shown in Plate VIII-28 through VIII-31. The miniature in Plate VIII-28 is reproduced from the psalter made for Saint Louis very early in the second half of the thirteenth century and illustrates the dream of Jacob: "And he dreamed, and behold a ladder set up on the earth, and the top of it reached to heaven: and behold the angels

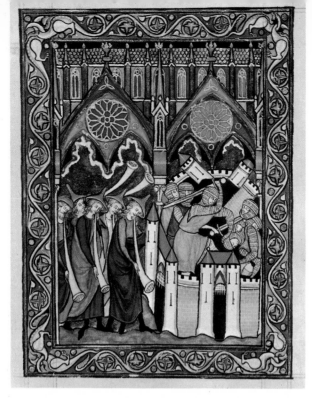

VIII-29. *Joshua's Sack of the City of Jericho,* miniature from the Psalter of St. Louis.

VIII-30. Miniature from the Psalter of Blanche of Castile (1230).

VIII-31. Page from the Breviary of Belleville, illuminated by Jean Pucelle (c. 1325).

of God ascending and descending on it" (Gen. 28:12). The architectural framework, not surprisingly, resembles that of Sainte-Chapelle. Plate VIII-29, a miniature from the same psalter, shows Joshua's armies in crusaders' armor, sacking the city of Jericho. A miniature (Plate VIII-30) from the personal psalter of Blanche of Castile, the mother of Saint Louis and the administrator of France while her son journeyed eastward to revive the Crusaders' Kingdom of Jerusalem, depicts two religious episodes: the apparition of Christ to Mary Magdalen, and the incredulity of "Doubting" Thomas.

The linear possibilities presented by manuscript painting were much greater than those of glass painting. As miniaturists developed their meticulous skills, the magnificence of their manuscripts increased. They delighted in making detailed reproductions of the intricacies of military dress and the splendors of contemporary fashion. Flowers and fruit, birds and animals began to creep about the borders of the pages, and scenes unfolded at a lively pace in front of burnished gold or sumptuously patterned backgrounds. An example of fourteenth-century refinement in French manuscript painting is seen in Plate VIII-31 in a page taken from the Breviary of Belleville, executed by the famous illuminator, Jean Pucelle, in about 1325.

The importance of tapestry work grew rapidly along with the new taste for decorative luxury. The Parisian workshops are considered the most important of those of the fourteenth century, but they were later surpassed by those patronized by Mahant d'Artois at Arras. The masterpieces of this period were the Apocalypse tapestries of Angers, commissioned by the Duke of Anjou, brother of King Charles V. Designed by Jean de Bruges and executed by

VIII-33. *Madonna and Child.* French ivory, Parisian School (early fourteenth century).

VIII-32. **Detail from an du Angers Apocalypse tapestry (end of fourteenth century).** (*pages 118–119*)

Nicolas Bataille, they were completed by the end of the fourteenth century. An episode from the Apocalyptic vision of Saint John is seen in Plate VIII-32: after the appearance from the sea of a lionlike beast with seven heads, ten horns, and ten crowns, and before whom all men kneel, another beast springs from the earth with the power to bring down fire from the heavens. (John, who is portrayed witnessing the scene at the left, had originally specified two horns "like those of a ram," but the designer has indulged in artistic license.)

Small portable objects such as carved ivories helped spread the French Gothic style across Europe. Elegant figures of the Virgin and Child (see Plate VIII-33) were much sought after, as were exquisite articles for everyday use such as brooches, sheaths, book covers, or hairpins. The two ivory pieces which served as the ends of boxes, like women's compacts, in Plate VIII-34 are representative of the Parisian School in the first half of the fourteenth century; aristocratic pursuits such as chess and falconry, seen here, provided favorite decorative themes for workers in ivory relief.

The masters of the Gothic period, like the architects of later ages, traveled constantly from country to country, carrying out new commissions, diffusing their skills, and perfecting and teaching new techniques. A vital document that has survived from this period is the so-called *Album* of Villard de Honnecourt, a notebook compiled by a French architect who traveled through France, Flanders, Switzerland, and Hungary. Villard noted down architectural features he admired, structural problems and their solutions, designs for church furniture, and mathematical formulae. It was architects like Villard de Honnecourt who also helped to spread the Gothic style throughout Europe.

VIII-34. Ivory case ends, Parisian School (first half of fourteenth century).

The Gothic Period: Germany, England, Spain, and Italy

GERMANY IN THE EARLY THIRTEENTH CENTURY remained the stronghold of the Romanesque tradition. When the Gothic influence began to make itself felt in religious architecture, two distinct groups of churches emerged: There were churches such as Saint Elizabeth at Marburg and Cologne Cathedral, which were basically French buildings transplanted to Germany and which indicate the extent of French influence on architecture. And there were cathedrals such as those at Limburg and at Magdeburg, representing a transition from Romanesque into Gothic, where individual French Gothic features were grafted onto predominantly Romanesque structures. It is thus not uncommon to find in a German church a Romanesque nave terminated by a Gothic east end, or a Gothic ribbed vault supported by massive Romanesque walls; at Romanesque Bamberg Cathedral (Plates IX-1, IX-2) the Gothic towers are clearly inspired by those of Laon Cathedral in France.

One of the most remarkable achievements of the German architects working in the Gothic period is the church dedicated to Saint Elizabeth of Hungary at Marburg (1235–1283). Elizabeth, daughter of the King of Hungary, was canonized in 1235 and her church became an extremely popular pilgrimage center. Though, as we said earlier, the church of Saint Elizabeth was basically a French building, it made one particular innovation that marked a vitally significant departure in Gothic construction and influenced the development of the Gothic style not only in Germany but in

IX-1. Bamberg Cathedral (begun 1186, consecrated 1237).

121

IX-2. Central nave of the Bamberg Cathedral.

IX-3. Church of the Virgin at Lubeck on the Baltic coast (1251–1300).

eastern Europe and as far away as England: all its aisles were the same height as the nave, with large windows that gave an impression of spaciousness and light. This new "hall church," which is a literal translation from the German *Hallenkirche,* was soon to be adopted by the religious order of the Teutonic Knights, who were primarily a preaching confraternity. The hall church was to become increasingly popular from the end of the thirteenth century on, and it remained the most common style in German religious architecture.

Hall churches constructed entirely of brick were a development almost entirely confined to certain areas of Germany; in the northern and eastern regions the sandy soil of the Baltic made stone an extremely expensive building material. Among the finest of these brick hall churches is the Church of the Virgin at Lubeck (*c.* 1251–1300), shown in Plate IX-3.

In the first half of the thirteenth century,

German Gothic sculpture flourished with an amazing richness and variety. Local styles were welded to imported French innovations, and this new synthesis proved to be a mature and original creation. In the sculpture of Naumburg and Magdeburg, this style developed an unprecedented degree of expressiveness. Funeral effigies and the figures of donors and saints were sculpted with a penetrating compassion and a deep insight into individual character. Gothic tomb figures such as those in Plates IX-4–IX-6 mark the transition of sculpture toward a revival of the Roman art of portraiture; the inner life of the soul was to be increasingly portrayed by facial expression.

German Gothic artists moved along completely new and original paths in the later thirteenth century and throughout the fourteenth century, far from the withdrawn dignity of the early French sculptors. The draperies in which the figures were clothed,

IX-4. Funeral effigies on the tombs of the margraves of Hesse, descendants of Saint Elizabeth of Hungary, (1235–1283), at the Church of Saint Elizabeth at Marburg.

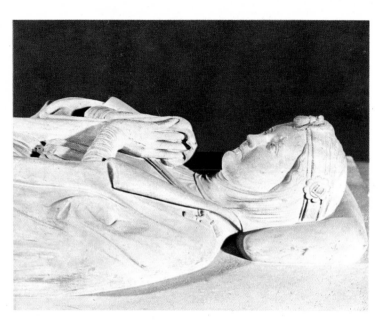

IX-5. Effigy from the tomb of Henry the Lion in Brunswick Cathedral (thirteenth century).

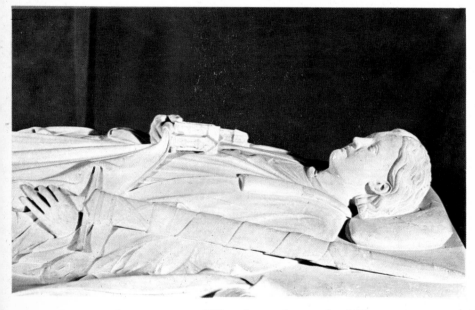

IX-6. Effigy from the tomb of Henry the Lion in Brunswick Cathedral (thirteenth century)

for example, were whipped into imaginative new rhythms suggesting vigorous movement.

Figure sculpture played a prominent part in the interior of German churches, especially in the large screens that have survived, and some of the most arresting sculptures are to be found at the cathedrals of Bamberg and Naumburg, two of the greatest masterpieces of the whole Gothic style. The works at these cathedrals give evidence of close artistic links with the great school of sculpture based in the cathedral workshops at Rheims in northeastern France, and in fact, the unknown masters who created them may have been trained at Rheims. However, the Germans brought to the Rheims style a sense of high emotional drama and unusual expressiveness. The statue known as *The Rider of Bamberg* (Plate IX-7) shows a slender yet forceful figure whose meaning still remains obscure. In the tympanum of the Portal of the Princes at Bamberg Cathedral appears a startling interpretation of the Last Judgment (Plates IX-8 and IX-9) where the contrasting facial expressions of the blessed and the damned are remarkably realistic in their intense joy or hysterical horror.

In the figures sculpted at Strasbourg Cathedral the facial expressions are lifelike to a degree unapproached by any Gothic sculpture in France (see Plate IX-10). The sculptors of the earlier workshop, who carved the choir screen and the serene figures of the Church (Plate IX-11) and the Synagogue at Strasbourg Cathedral, were obviously aware of the schools of Chartres and Rheims, but they managed to create their own purely personal style. Similar tendencies are evident in sculpture on a small scale, particularly in wood, which was a very popular material in Germany. The weeping Virgin became a familiar theme for

IX-8. *The Souls of the Damned,* detail from *The Last Judgment,* Bamberg Cathedral.

IX-7. *The Rider of Bamberg,* Bamberg Cathedral (1233–1237).

IX-9. Detail of *The Last Judgment* from the tympanum of the Portal of the Princes, Bamberg Cathedral.

IX-10. *The Last Supper* and *The Capture of Christ,* details from the tympanum of the main portal of Strasbourg Cathedral (1280).

IX-11. *The Church Triumphant,* statue from the south transept doorway at Strasbourg Cathedral (c. 1220–1225).

wood sculpture, an example is shown in Plate IX-12. A less emotional quality, following in the French tradition, was shown in small painted wooden statues, probably intended for private devotion in a family chapel, such as in the one in Plate IX-13. The statue in Plate IX-14, carved in about 1330, probably in the region of the middle Rhine, symbolizes learning and has no religious significance.

German Gothic metalwork, from the very first decades of the Gothic era, produced works of great sensitivity and accomplishment, and only because of the size of its creations should it be considered a minor art. Candelabra, baptismal fonts, altar frontals, hangings for the front of altars, and reliquaries were the most common products of the period. The raised sculpted figures that decorated these objects were

IX-13. *Madonna and Child,* painted wooden statue (late thirteenth century). Germanisches Nationalmuseum, Nuremburg.

IX-14. The Teacher (1330).

IX-12. *Mater Dolorosa,* or *The Virgin of the Sorrows,* painted wooden sculpture, Upper Saxony (*c.* 1230).

IX-15. **Detail from the reliquary of Saint Elizabeth of Hungary, copper gilt and precious stones (thirteenth century).**

IX-16. The Crown of Henry (*c.* 1270–1280).

often of such high quality that, in their dramatic power and technical accomplishment, they compare favorably with much larger stone statues. The same holds true in enamel work, for the products of the German Gothic enamel foundries rivaled the finest work of the Romanesque period. A detail from the reliquary of Saint Elizabeth of Hungary is shown in Plate IX-15; this casket, in copper gilt and precious stones, was made in the thirteenth century and in 1236 received the relics of the Saint. Another example, the magnificent Crown of Henry in Plate IX-16, was made between 1270 and 1280 and probably originated in an Upper Rhenish workshop.

Manuscript illumination was another area where German Gothic art flourished. Artists of the thriving German schools generally preferred to draw their subject matter from the daily life and occupations of the court and nobility, and the tendency, in the thirteenth century, was toward a great richness of color and elegant, decorative forms. The artists illustrated courtly romances and tales of chivalry, heroism, and unrequited love. One of these has survived, from the area of Strasbourg, a luxuriously illuminated manuscript of the poem *Parzival* (about the hero known also as Parsifal or Sir Percivale); its style, as can be seen in Plate IX-17, shows an intimate knowledge of the Psalter of Saint Louis.

England assimilated the new Gothic style with astonishing rapidity. At first French influence dominated, as can be seen from Canterbury Cathedral; soon, however, English masons began to create a national style of true originality.

At Durham Cathedral, the crowning masterpiece of Anglo-Norman Romanesque architecture, certain architectural elements appeared that were later to be adopted, though with some modifications, as outstanding features of the pure Gothic style. Pointed arches and ribbed vaults were both used at Durham, but they had been of decorative rather than structural importance; the massive walls bore no resemblance whatsoever to the light, soaring constructions of the Gothic architects. The urge to develop these innovations and to give them a wider architectural scope came directly from France; indeed it was a French architect, William of Sens, who laid down the main lines of England's first purely Gothic cathedral, at Canterbury. William of Sens had been chosen by the chapter of the cathedral from a number of candidates, and his term of office as master of the cathedral works was carefully chronicled by a resident monk known as Gervase of Canterbury.

IX-17. **Miniature from the illuminated poem** *Parzival*, **by Wolfram von Eschenbach** (*c.* 1228–1236).

The choir at Canterbury Cathedral (Plate IX-18) has a predominantly Gothic appearance and bears signs of a close contact with the new structural features originating in the Île-de-France such as sexpartite (six-part) vaulting (Plate VIII-4) and "open" walls that allowed for large stained-glass windows. But this dependence on contemporary French models was not destined

IX-18. The choir of Canterbury Cathedral, looking toward the apse (1175–1179).

to play either an important or a lasting role in the development of an English Gothic style. French Gothic structural elements continued to be used solely for decorative purposes, and the sense of extreme height and lightness characteristic of French architecture was never sought by the English. Though the English continued to draw, from time to time, on the French Gothic, their spirit was to be an independent one. What they achieved was always a purely English synthesis.

Lincoln Cathedral, the reconstruction of which was begun in 1192, is a purely English Gothic building. The new work at Lincoln was the inspiration of its saintly bishop, Hugh of Avalon, and his master architect, Geoffrey de Noyers. The height of Lincoln Cathedral does not match that of any of its contemporary French counterparts, such as the cathedrals at Chartres, Bourges, and Soissons, but it is much longer; two transepts, instead of only one, lie midway between the apse and the entrance to the cathedral. The structural rhythm of Lincoln is slow and majestic, with notably broad arcades in the nave. The arcade arches (Plate IX-19) are only moderately pointed, further emphasizing the length and horizontal character of the interior. It was in the vaulting that Lincoln made its main architectural contribution, however: its complicated system of vaulting represents a fundamental advance in the Gothic style. Romanesque elements appear incorporated around the doors in Lincoln's facade (Plate IX-20), but the cathedral front is primarily a vast decorated stone screen that bears little apparent relation to the interior of the cathedral.

The first phase of English Gothic was soon to be followed by a more evolved Gothic style. This second phase had its origins in the reconstruction of West-

IX-19. The "Angel" choir of Lincoln Cathedral (1255–1280).

IX-20. Facade of Lincoln Cathedral (*c.* 1140–1200).

minster Abbey and in new work undertaken at York. At Westminster (Plate IX-21), French decorative details were combined with the most advanced structural techniques of the age. Conceived by Edward III as a sumptuous shrine for the remains of his ancestors, Westminster Abbey was in many respects consciously imitative of Sainte-Chapelle in Paris.

The next phase in the development of Gothic architecture in England is generally termed the Decorated Style. Basically it consisted of a new concentration on elements that had already made their appearance in English Gothic architecture. Naturalistic motifs—animals, flowers, leaves, and fruit—played an increasingly important role in the decoration of church

IX-21. The sanctuary of Westminster Abbey, (thirteenth-century) London.

IX-22. Octagonal lantern or architectural opening above intersection of transept and nave, Ely Cathedral (completed early in the second quarter of the fourteenth century).

IX-23. A view of the nave looking east in Wells Cathedral (1184–1339).

interiors. Found on capitals, above arches, and between pilasters, they completely replaced the stylized patterns that had been a characteristic feature of English architecture during the Romanesque period. These more imaginative and sculptural decorative elements gave the interiors an organic quality. Even the moldings on the arcade arches became more complex. Moreover, the structural developments that enabled windows to be larger in area resulted in a profuse flowering of tracery (lacy decorative carved stone) into rich and fantastic patterns. Tracery began to simulate natural forms in its curving lines, and eventually it covered the whole surface of the vaults.

Between 1280 and 1340 English Gothic was the most sophisticated and exciting architecture in Europe and contributed some of the most original achievements of the Gothic period, such as the reconstruction of Exeter, the superb hall church at Bristol, the octagon of Ely Cathedral (Plate IX-22), and the east end of Wells Cathedral (Plate IX-23). (The great bracing arch that dominates the nave of Wells is a later addition.)

The third and final phase of English

Gothic architecture, now generally termed the Perpendicular Style, began in the first half of the fourteenth century. It originated from a synthesis of various elements developed in France in the previous century.

The Perpendicular Style is basically an amplification of many features already present in English architecture. For example, the Perpendicular Style increased the size of windows. The walls became immense sheets of delicately tinted grisaille glass, seemingly supported only by webs of diaphanous tracery; light and color, now even more than before, filled the cathedrals and contributed to the spiritual atmosphere of their interiors.

The trend toward a dissolving of the wall mass into stone tracery and glass was also to stimulate church-building, making this the most productive period in English Gothic architecture. The whole structure of the buildings was pared down and the interior moldings became more geometrically conceived and intricate. All these elements contributed to the sense of verticality that was the essence of the Perpendicular Style; the west facade of Winchester Cathedral (Plate IX-24) is a good example.

In England, the violence of the Reformation in the 16th century brought about the almost complete destruction of many facade sculptures of the great cathedrals. Throughout the English Gothic period, sculpture was subordinated to architecture to a far greater extent than it was in Europe. It seems undeniable, however, that English taste leaned to purely decorative sculpture, incorporating flowers, foliage, and animals. Apart from the sculptured exterior of Wells Cathedral (Plate IX-25), there is little trace of monumental sculpture on English cathedral facades. Monumental sculpture during this period is largely con-

IX-24. **The west facade of Winchester Cathedral.**

fined to funeral effigies such as the figure of King John in Worcester Cathedral (Plate IX-26).

Manuscript illumination in England during the Gothic era developed greatly in scope and expressiveness between 1250 and 1340. After that it swiftly deteriorated with the collapse of the prolific East Anglian School noted for its marginal decorations of secular nature. Between 1250 and 1300, English manuscript illumination was closely in touch with developments in French miniature painting. A page from the Psalter of Robert de Lisle, known as the Arundel Psalter (Plate IX-27), though of a slightly later period, shows a close knowledge of contemporary work in northeastern France. Illuminated Apocalypses were in fashion at

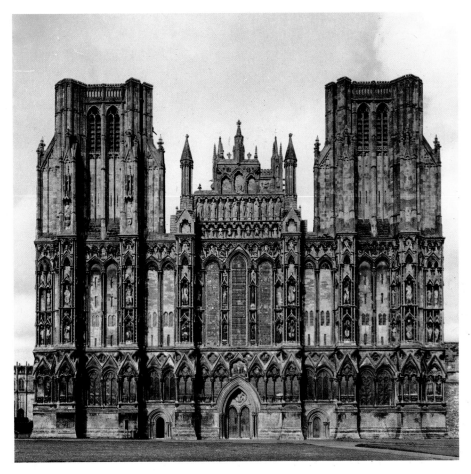

IX-25. Wells Cathedral (1184–1339).

IX-26. Effigy of King John in Worcester Cathedral (*c.* 1225–1230).

IX-27. **Page from the Arundel Psalter** (*c.* 1339).

IX-28. **Miniatures from an illustrated Apocalypse (late fifteenth century).**

IX-29. **English Gothic embroidery depicting the tree of Jesse (fourteenth century).**

the time, and English artists made their own contributions here, among the finest being the Apocalypse in Trinity College, Cambridge (Plate IX-28). The broad surfaces and bright, flat colors are characteristic of the English style.

One of the most famous products of medieval England was its extraordinarily fine needlework, which became so renowned that it was simply known as *Opus Anglicanum*, literally "English work." A detail of an elaborately embroidered religious vestment, depicting the tree of Jesse, appears in Plate IX-29. (The genealogy of Christ according to the Gospel of Saint Matthew was usually illustrated as a tree springing from

the side of Jesse, father of David, and culminating in a figure of the Virgin Mary cradling the Holy Infant in her arms.)

In Spain, the introduction of the Gothic style was due, to a considerable extent, to her close and direct connections with France. Saint Louis's mother, Blanche of Castile, a devoted patron of the arts, was Spanish. Many French priests became bishops in Spain. And many pilgrimage roads threaded their tortuous way from France into Spain across the rugged Pyrenees, acting as the main channels of cultural influence and exchange. French architects and sculptors from such places as Rheims, Amiens, Bourges, and Le Mans are certainly known to have worked at the cathedrals of Burgos, León, and Toledo, which constitute three of the primary monuments of Spanish Gothic architecture. In fact, the south of France and northern Spain in the Gothic period may be considered as forming a single artistic entity, bound together by politics, religion, commerce, and the dynastic alliances between ruling families.

Spain in this period was also an embattled frontier of Christianity, defending herself against the Arabs, who were still occupying parts of the peninsula; and the Arabs were accomplished builders with a long tradition behind them. Thus, at the beginning of the Gothic period, Spanish architecture was also in contact with Arab structural and decorative elements.

IX-30. The west facade of Burgos Cathedral (1221–1567).

The first genuinely Gothic cathedrals in Spain are found in the north, in the cities, mentioned above, of Burgos, León, and Toledo. All three show close affinities with French churches, and in particular, the cathedrals at Burgos (Plate IX-30) and Toledo show the marked influence of the French Bourges Cathedral, which was to have a profoundly stimulating and far-reaching effect on the development of Spanish Gothic architecture. As this might indicate, the architecture of at least the early Gothic period in Spain was primarily imitative; the early architecture reveals nothing fundamentally new in the Gothic style. León Cathedral, for example, is in many ways a crude reproduction of Rheims by provincial Spanish craftsmen. Other centers in Spain tried, in turn, to imitate the architectural achievement of the three northern Spanish cathedrals, but many of these smaller buildings, often planned by foreign architects and executed by local masons, are only unskillful interpretations of the sophisticated style imported from France.

Spanish sculptors were also imitative in the beginning. In subject matter and style, they mimicked French representations of the Last Judgment and Christ in Majesty. The workmanship is less refined than that in the sculpture of the great French cathedrals, but it has an exciting vigor and an individuality that were to become characteristic of later Spanish developments.

Only gradually did Spanish sculptors gain full mastery of the art in which French sculptors were already so highly skilled; they were most successful in the production of small-scale works. Apart from the huge figure sculptures on the cathedrals, there was a considerable output of small statuettes of wood (particularly in the Catalan work-

IX-31. *Madonna and Child,* carved and painted wood, Spanish Gothic (thirteenth century).

IX-32. Statuette in colored stone representing an unknown pope in an attitude of benediction, **Spanish Gothic (thirteenth century).**

shops) and of colored stone (Plates IX-31, IX-32). Catalonia also was noted for its vigorous and independent school of painting. The painting of Navarre and Castile, however, was more strongly influenced by the French court style. A fragment of a fresco illustrating the annunciation to the shepherds (Plate IX-33), painted about 1359 by the Master of Olite, shows, in its delicate colors and fastidious drawing, an awareness of French miniature painting of the fourteenth century.

IX-33. *The Annunciation to the Shepherds,* fragment from a Spanish Gothic fresco by the **Master of Olite** (*c.* 1359).

In thirteenth-century Italy, the past still exerted considerable influence upon the arts. Byzantine techniques were still widespread in painting, while architecture remained fundamentally Romanesque. Gothic features and structural innovations were introduced principally by the Cistercians, who erected churches in Italy that conformed strictly to French models. One of the first and most imitated of these Cistercian foundations was the Abbey of Fossanova (Plate IX-34), which was followed by those at Vasamari and by San Galgano at Siena. The typical Cistercian ground plan consisted of a Latin cross (the cross as we usually know it; a Greek cross has arms of equal length and can fit into a square or circle), terminated by a square-ended choir at the east end. This plan, distinguished by the clarity of its volumes and by the austere, almost Romanesque simplicity of its interior, was used in a large number of Italian churches built during the thirteenth century. Easily copied because of its extreme simplicity, the Cistercian architectural formula did not tax the technical capacity of even the most provincial Italian masons.

In southern Italy, an important and distinct stylistic school was created by the architects working at the court of Emperor Frederick II. Their achievement is represented by a number of sturdy fortresses (see Plate IX-35) most often built on symmetrical ground plans and placed in strategic locations all over the countryside. The principles on which these fortresses were built probably derived from a study of Roman and Sassanid (Persian) forts and from a knowledge of warfare gained from the Crusades.

The city of Florence offers some good examples of Gothic religious and secular architecture. The churches of Santa Croce

IX-34. **Nave of the Abbey of Fossanova,** (1208) Tuscany.

IX-35. **Castel del Monte,** (1240–1246) Apulia.

(begun in 1252) and Santa Maria del Fiore (1296–1887, Plate IX-36), colossal in size, recall the Early Christian basilicas in their extreme austerity and solemn distribution of space. And the secular Palazzo della Signoria (Plate IX-37), known also as the Palazzo Vecchio ("Old Palace"), an administrative building similar to a town hall, exemplifies a building style typical of many Italian cities of the time. Like its many counterparts, it is characterized by severe geometric lines and a rectangular tower.

Four exceptional Italian Gothic artists heralded the Renaissance of the next century—the painter Giotto 1266/7–1337), the architect Arnolfo de Cambio (died *c.* 1302), and the sculptors Nicola and Giovanni Pisano, who were father and son (*c.* 1220/5–1284 and 1245/50–1314, respectively); their revolutionary work, while falling chronologically into the Gothic period, has more bearing on Renaissance than on Gothic art.

On the whole, however, early thirteenth-century Italian painting seemed unable to slip from the stranglehold of Byzantine formalism. Strict rules continued to govern the scheme of religious scenes, dictating the garments of the principles, the gestures, and even the colors. Mosaic work and sculpture similarly display a cold academic quality and lack both sensitivity and imaginative insight.

If we were to seek a center for Gothic

art, we would probably have to point to France; however, in some of the minor arts and in certain regional syntheses, the other countries of Europe made outstanding contributions, and we should thus recognize Germany, England, Spain, and Italy for their specific achievements in the Gothic period.

IX-36. Santa Maria del Fiore, (1296–1887) Florence.

IX-37. Palazzo della Signoria, (1298–1344) Florence. Interior (1296–1436).

THE CONCLUDING PHASE of the Gothic style is known as International Gothic and had its origins at the French and Burgundian courts. As the new style spread to societies across the breadth of Europe, it soon became difficult to distinguish the art of one country from that of another.

Two qualities characterize the style of International Gothic: an overwhelming emphasis upon detail and an almost excessive love of luxury, elegance, and tangible richness. "Courtly" taste prevailed, and in the decorative arts we find a booming production in tapestries and textiles, statuettes and jewelry; we find extraordinary book illustrations and *objets d'art* (art objects) such as the Parisian gold and mother-of-pearl saltcellar in the form of a ship and mermaid shown in Plate X-1. The demand for precious ornaments, especially jewelry, was incessant, and among the more prosperous classes it became the fashion to have one's portrait set in a medallion. In such portraits the artists frequently revealed a keen observation of character, as may be seen in the example reproduced in Plate X-2.

As literacy spread among European aristocracies, a new field of patronage was opened to book illuminators. Books were now illustrated with scenes of contemporary life, and artists were encouraged to depict a world of indolence, of feasting, dancing, and hunting parties. In the Middle Ages it had been the custom to decorate calendars with the particular activity of each month, such as harvesting or sowing. The illuminators of the new calendars began to study their environment. They recorded both interior and exterior scenes with an inquisi-

X-1. Parisian saltcellar in the shape of a ship (*c.* 1482).

X-2. French portrait medallion (*c.* 1440).

X-3 Miniature of a prophet from the Psalter of the Duke of Berry (1380–1385).

always occupied a prominent position. Throughout the Middle Ages, French miniature workshops had poured out a stream of exquisitely drawn and colored books for their royal patrons. But with the later advances made in printing, there appeared a sudden abundance of secular, or nonreligious, works: books of moral purpose and tales of courtly romance, such as *Chess Moralised* or *The Romance of Alexander.*

With the advent of the International Gothic style, the pictorial techniques of telling a story changed. Instead of employing familiar and traditional symbols as before, artists now sought to record a profusion of detail in order to achieve greater accuracy and realism. The greatest illuminators of the late Gothic period worked at the court of the Duke of Berry at Bourges and at the court of the Duke of Burgundy at Dijon. Among those who painted for the Duke of Berry were André Beauneveu (see Plate X-3), who excelled in both manuscript illumination and stone carving, and the famous yet mysterious Jacquemart de Hesdin (Plate X-4), who was purely an illuminator, and whose work appears in a Book of Hours commissioned by the Duke. (A Book of Hours contains prayers to be said at certain prescribed times of the day.)

Most famous of all late Gothic manuscripts is another of the Duke's Books of Hours, this one known as the *Très Riches Heures du Duc de Berry.* It was made by the Limbourg brothers and was left unfinished following their death in the plague of 1416. This manuscript is the finest example of the International Gothic style in painting (see Plates X-5, X-6). The splendid elegance of the court is depicted with a fascinating accuracy, and the leisure activities of its inhabitants take place in complex landscapes composed with a studious obser-

tive accuracy and a growing awareness of spatial perspective. In their manuscript illuminations, they devoted great attention to the representation of detail, to the textural qualities of sumptuous silks and brocades, to the glint of silver and the sparkle of jeweled costumes.

The occupations of man's daily life were also captured with a new truthfulness and conviction. Animals and birds, which had previously decorated only the borders of pages, were now incorporated in greater profusion in the main miniatures themselves. The world of natural appearances became again the preoccupation and source of inspiration for artists.

In the courts of the French king and nobility, manuscript illumination had

x-4. *Virgin of the Supplication,* page from the double frontispiece of *The Book of Hours,* possibly by André Beauneveu (1404–1409).

vation of natural detail. The Limbourg brothers also managed to extend their interest outside court circles to the occupations of farmers and laborers, and many of their illuminations show peasants working in the fields. Even these less elaborate scenes are captured with the same delicacy and attention to minute detail that is found in the courtly scenes and that, indeed, characterizes the entire *Très Riches Heures.*

Clothing, often so carefully depicted in these miniatures, was in itself an important facet of the International Gothic style. Rank was reflected in the way one dressed; in Burgundy the merchant princes dressed in a prescribed costume, just as peasants, artisans, and servants did. Jews wore the pointed hats seen in the illustrations from the Psalter of Saint Louis in Plates VIII-27 and VIII-28, knights wore specific colors to

X-5. *The Month of June,* miniature from the *Très Riches Heures du Duc de Berry,* by the Limbourg brothers, (*c.* 1416).

X-6. *The Month of April,* miniature from the *Très Riches Heures.*

advertise the progress of their love affairs, and even lepers and hangmen were expected to attire themselves in a specific manner. Without belaboring the point, we might say that fashion seemed to follow the typical style and line of Gothic architecture—costumes were long and slender, with pointed hats, sleeves, and shoes in place of pointed arches, and blazing jewelry in place of stained-glass windows. However, during this period men and women became so intrigued with fashion that costume threatened to become a social obsession. "Folly bells" trimmed the clothes of smart men and women alike, and hennins, ladies' pointed hats, sometimes towered as high as three or four feet above their heads. Pointed shoes became so long that they roused considerable consternation; it was finally decreed that dukes and princes could wear wire-reinforced pointed toes and that their shoes might measure a total of two and a half times the length of the foot, while the lower aristocracy, the merely rich, and the commoners had to satisfy themselves with pointed toes of diminishing proportions in keeping with their descending ranks. Such exaggeration in styles brought down the wrath of the clergy, and Franciscan monks went so far as to refuse absolution to women who wore long trains.

International Gothic art has given us a faithful record of the costume of the period; Plate X-7, for example, a mid-fifteenth-century tapestry from Belgium shows a typically dressed couple of noble rank. An allegorical figure of Love, dressed in white, accompanied by Heart in full armor, encounters red-eyed Jealousy in a charming detail (Plate X-8) from a miniature by the Master of King René, Duke of Anjou, that illustrates the chivalric *Livre de Coeur d'Amour Épris* (The Book of the Heart Seized by Love); Love's white cos-

X-7. Courtly scene tapestry from Tournai (mid-fifteenth century).

X-8. *Love and Heart Encounter Jealousy.*

X-9. *Paradise Garden,* panel painting by the Master of the Paradise Garden (*c.* 1420).

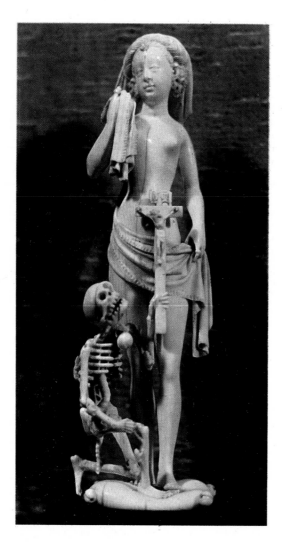

X-10. *Vanity*, French ivory figure, late Gothic.

tume symbolizes hopeful longing, for he has now declared his affections, while Heart's red trimmings signify his position as "a vassal of love."

The breathless attention paid by society to these elaborate conventions reveals a shallowness and preoccupation with trivia that was totally foreign to the original spiritual impulse behind Christian art. The enormous charm of the *Paradise Garden* (Plate X-9) cannot be denied, yet the emotional content of this painting, in which the Virgin is presented as a doll-like princess reading a book in an enchanting garden, seems negligible when compared with that of the Virgin and Child of the catacombs (Plate I-7). The strength of Christian art had always depended upon a depth of spiritual feeling, and in the tide of materialism that rose to inundate the Gothic age, too many people overlooked the moral of such decorative and exquisitely terrifying works as the ivory figure of Vanity seen in Plate X-10 who mindlessly ignores both the inevitability of death and the spiritual message of Christ. Forgotten indeed was the admonition of Matthew to the early Christians: "Lay not up for yourselves treasures upon earth . . . But lay up for yourselves treasures in heaven . . . For where your treasure is, there will your heart be also."

LIST OF ILLUSTRATIONS

Autographs

Teresa Curcuru & Good Luck in the future Love ya

Paula Curcuru Good luck with finals Love ya

John Curcuru Dad Love ya with all my heart

Victor Olivero Love ya very much

Joe Costa, AT, Love ya - Good Luck in 7th

JoAnn Thompson Love ya Glad I'm your baby sitter

Kathy Curcuru Mom.

Good Luck I love you Ann-Marie

INDEX